PRAISE FOR MARK DAVID GERSON

The MoonQuest: A True Fantasy

An evocative and emotionally moving tale...

MIDWEST BOOK REVIEW

An exceptional, timeless novel...

MINDQUEST REVIEW OF BOOKS

Coaching, Classes & Workshops

Mark David is a master...one of the great teachers!

REV. MARY OMWAKE, UNITY OF MAUI;
LEADERSHIP COUNCIL, ASSOCIATION FOR GLOBAL NEW THOUGHT

An absolute life-changing experience,
above and beyond my expectations.

JOANNA TSCHUDY, ST. LOUIS, MISSOURI

I can't believe how easy Mark David has made it.
No more writer's block!

AZUREL EFRON, SEDONA, ARIZONA

ALSO BY MARK DAVID GERSON

*The Voice of the Muse Companion:
Guided Meditation for Writers*

THE
VOICE
OF THE
MUSE

Answering the Call to Write

MARK DAVID GERSON

LightLINES™
MEDIA

Printed in the United States of America.

Published by LightLines Media
223 N. Guadalupe St., Unit 171
Santa Fe, NM 87501

www.LightLinesMedia.com

First LightLines Edition: 2008

Interior book design: Groundwork Design
Cover design: Richard Crookes
Author photo: Kathleen Messmer

10 9 8 7 6 5 4 3 2 1

Publisher's Cataloging-in-Publication data

Gerson, Mark David.
    The voice of the muse : answering the call to write / Mark David Gerson.
    p. cm.
    ISBN 978-0-9795475-5-3
1. Authorship. 2. Creative writing. 3. Spiritual life. 4. Creation (Literary, artistic, etc.).
5. Creative ability. 6. Creative writing--Problems, exercises, etc. I. Title.

PN145 .G45 2008
808.0220--dc22   2007906086

Writing is alchemy...truly a tool of wizards,
witches and sorcerers.
It's the magic wand, the incantation, the wave
of the hand that transforms all...

MARK DAVID GERSON

To the creator alchemist in us all

Table of Contents

Appreciation

My deepest gratitude flows to Carole H. Leckner, who once upon a time a long time ago repeatedly asked me to teach even as I repeatedly said no, and to a dream presence named Beth, who urged me to overcome my fear and say yes. Without them, I would be neither writing nor teaching today.

Many others have contributed to this project, directly and indirectly: Marisha Diaz, Sander Dov Freedman and Karen Weaver, my A-1 support team in all my endeavors; Joan Cerio, who unintentionally propelled these words into print; A'alia Golden, who encouraged me through the book's early drafts and suggested the title; Geri O'Hare for her gentle and prayerful nurturing; Rev. Mary Omwake and Unity of Maui for their mana, kokua and aloha during my years of teaching there; and my daughter, Guinevere, always an inspiration.

Thanks, too, to all my students, clients and workshop participants over the years: The powerful words you penned in response to mine helped persuade me to set down on these pages all we experienced together.

No honor roll would be complete without mentioning Michael Hice, my publicist; Richard Crookes and Peter McGrath, this book's accomplished and patient designers; and Cynthia Fritz, whose eagle-eyed copyediting corrected many an unfortunate phrase.

As an unrepentant believer in the assistive power of place, I also acknowledge the many sacred landscapes whose energy and spirit contributed to this project: the volcanic highlands of Kohala and Mauna Kea on the Big Island of Hawaii; Maui's Kahalawai and Haleakala foothills; Albuquerque's Sandia Mountains; the red rocks and cliffs of Sedona, Arizona; and the enchanted earth, waters and skies of places too numerous to mention.

If much of this book was penned in a car in Hawaii, most of it was organized and revised in these welcoming cafés and bookstores: Ravenheart Coffee and Lemuria Calling in Sedona, Satellite Coffee in Albuquerque, and Borders stores in Santa Fe and Albuquerque, New Mexico.

Finally, to my Muse: Thank you for your annoying persistence and loving support with this and all my writing.

1.

Getting Started

Start a huge, foolish project, like Noah...

RUMI

Writing is like driving at night in the fog.
You can only see as far as your headlights, but
you can make the whole trip that way.

E.L. DOCTOROW

The Writer You Are

Whoever you are, you can write. Whether you've never penned a word, struggle with words or have written forever, you can write effortlessly, painlessly and freely. Whatever you believe about your talent, your skill, your imagination or your creativity, if it contains one ounce of doubt, let it go. You *are* a writer — of power, strength and substance. Repeat that. Aloud, if you dare.

> *I am a writer of power, strength and substance.*

Again:

> *I am a writer of power, strength and substance.*

One more time:

> *I am a writer of power, strength and substance.*

You can write. Coherently. Flowingly. Engagingly. You can write with ease, even if you believe yourself to be blocked...even if you don't yet know what to write. You can write in ways that touch others, that change yourself and the world.

You can because anyone can. Anyone can because free-flowing creativity is innate, coded into your genes, your cells, your DNA.

Whether you're a seasoned professional or just starting out, the concepts, inspiration and exercises in this book will initiate a flow of creativity that will, frankly, amaze you.

You doubt? I don't blame you. Once upon a time, I wouldn't have believed me either. Once upon a time, I felt blocked, doubted my creative ability, denied I had anything of value to contribute through my words.

"Oh," I would acknowledge after more than a decade of professional journalism, "I'm a skilled technician, an excellent grammarian and a clever manipulator of others' words and ideas. But creative? No way!"

That was once upon a time. Now, after fifteen years of working with and teaching the concepts in this book, I know I was wrong.

I didn't set out to write this book. It crept up on me when I wasn't looking, when I didn't know I was writing it.

Many of the essays in this volume began as journal entries, self-motivating vignettes penned during a time when I needed inspiration. Most were written during my eighteen months on the Big Island of Hawaii as I struggled through the early stages of a sequel to my novel, *The MoonQuest*, another book that had its way with me before I realized what I was creating.

Once I had amassed several notebooks of these inspirational pieces on writing, the voice of my Muse insisted I had the beginnings of a book and the creative wisdom to complete it.

I wrote *The Voice of the Muse* — and *The MoonQuest* — using the basic premise of my philosophy, what I call "writing on the Muse Stream." I call it the Muse Stream because I believe that when we surrender to our Muse, creativity pours through us as effortlessly as water in a free-flowing stream.

You'll read more about the Muse Stream in the pages that follow. In brief, however, it involves stilling the often-censorious personality mind, setting pen to paper and allowing the river of words to flow on their own undirected course, trusting the voyage of discovery inherent in all creative life.

Surrendering to the Muse Stream is about knowing that the book, poem, song, article or journal entry resides in some other realm and trusting enough to follow the pen as it spills onto the blank sheet the words, sentences, paragraphs and pages that will reveal its already existent form.

The skills you will learn here have less to do with outlines, marketability, plotting, form or vocabulary, although I will address some aspects of writing craft toward the end of the book. If, as I believe, your story (and I use that word to encompass all you would relate through your writing) already exists, the only skills you need to master involve listening, trusting, allowing and discerning.

The Muse Stream is, of course, well-suited to stream-of-consciousness jottings, disconnected scenes and journal-like vignettes. But it can do more for you...much more. You can write an entire book, if that is your vision and your choice. And you can begin it now, even if you don't yet know what your book is about.

However your Muse calls, the words lie within you. They hover in the shadows, longing to be noticed, yearning to be heard, aching to be shared.

Together, through this book, you and I will give them voice. It may not be the voice you planned or expected. It will be the voice of your power, carrying you to wherever you need to go.

Whether or not you know what you want to write, whether or not you seek to be published, begin by opening to the notion that whatever has drawn you to your page and these pages starts with you, with the call and voice of *your* Muse.

Ignore all external direction and all internal criticism. Pay no heed to what the "market will bear."

What the market seeks today may not be what it will seek when your book or story is complete. What your heart calls you to write in this moment may be just what others' hearts will cry out to read in two months, six months or a year.

When your Muse's call comes, you cannot know where it will take you... or why. All you can do is listen, follow and trust...and know that the voice will always speak the words you are ready to hear, the words you are ready to write. Go within. Trust that voice to guide you, moment by moment, word by word, breath by breath, on a journey of unfoldment, a journey into the experience of your creativity.

As you'll read often through these pages, there is no right way and no wrong way, only the way that works for you, in this moment. So use this book however you feel called to.

Flip to any page at random, trusting that the words you read are those you are ready to read, that the exercise or meditation to which you have been directed is the one that will serve you best that day. Or follow the book in sequence, traveling with me on the journey I was called upon to initiate, knowing that we travel together.

Either way, glance through *The Muse Stream* (Chapter 3) early in your meanderings and keep handy the tips listed in *If You Get Stuck* (page 32). Consider it your emergency roadside assistance kit.

Consider, too, starting a journal or notebook in which you record your impressions and experiences of this voyage of reawakening and rediscovery. If you are working on or toward a book, let this journal also be the place where you explore its ideas and directions, release your anxieties and frustrations and express gratitude and appreciation to the Muse whose call you have begun to answer.

Before you turn the page and launch your journey, though, you'll need a pen, an envelope and a couple of index cards or pieces of paper.

Have you got them? Yes? Then you're ready!

Preparing to Move Forward

Where are you now? Where are you now in your writing? In your life?

Where are you now that you chose to open this book — to this question, to this page?

Close your eyes and let a single word, phrase or sentence emerge that describes where you are in this moment. Don't second-guess it. Let it be whatever it is, however little conventional sense it seems to make.

When that word, phrase or sentence has bubbled up to your conscious mind, write it on your piece of paper or index card next to the question, "Where am I now?"

Don't judge it. Just let it be whatever it is, and record it.

Now, consider these questions...

What do you want from this book? What are your desires? Your expectations? Your preferences?

Where would you like to be on the last page of this book that you aren't now?

Take a few minutes and jot down a few notes on your piece of paper or index card. Record those desires, those expectations, those preferences. Let it be a few words, a few sentences or a few pages. Let it be whatever you need it to be. Let it express whatever you opened this book seeking.

When you're done, sign it, date it and place it in a sealed envelope. Secure it to the inside back cover of this book and forget about it.

You have set the wheels in motion. Now it's time to let them carry you to your destination.

2.

The Call

There are times when you have to obey a call
which is the highest of all.

GANDHI

Authentic writers write even if
there is little chance for them to be published; they
write because they cannot do otherwise.

ELI WIESEL

Have You Heard the Call?

Have you heard the call? Have you heard the call that thrills as it terrifies you? Have you heard the call to set something down on paper? To tell a story...one you think you do not know? To inspire others...in ways you do not yet understand?

Perhaps you fear the pen that stares at you across the desk, the blank screen that glares at you accusingly.

What does this Muse want of you? Why won't it go away?

It won't because it can't. It can't any more than you can ignore it.

As long as that siren sings to you, neither you nor it can rest until you answer. You know that. You know that or you wouldn't be reading these pages. You know that or this book wouldn't have leapt out and demanded your attention.

Your Muse, too, demands your attention. For you do have a story to tell. You have words to share, words that demand to be heard, words *you* need to hear.

It doesn't matter if you don't know what they are. That's why I'm here.

It doesn't matter that what you know or suspect of them scares you. That's also why I am here.

It doesn't matter that you don't know how to begin if you haven't begun, how to continue if you have already started or how to complete if you find yourself stuck part way through. That, too, is why I am here.

I am the author of this book. And I, too, hear the voice of the Muse, my Muse. It whispers to me, shouts at me and prompts me to release its words — our words — onto the page. It urges me to inspire and reassure you, to tell you that it's not only possible but safe to listen to the voice of your Muse and answer your call to write.

That's why I am here. That's why you are here. All you need to do to begin to heed that call is take a deep breath, turn the page and read on.

Your Words Made Manifest

When did the call first come? When did you know, as clearly as you know your face, that you had to write? When did you know that an imperative deeper than any you have known was crying out for you to express it in words? When did you know?

How long has it been? How long has it been since you heard that voice? How long until you acted? Have you acted? Or have you fled?

Whatever or whichever, the time is now to set pen to paper. You know it. You know it as surely and truly as you know that face in the mirror. It is the face that calls you to write. For you are your Muse, if you allow that to be...if you allow yourself to listen.

You listened, you say, and here you are: pen poised over a sea of nothingness, wondering where that ocean of stories is. Wonder no longer. That ocean resides in the inkwell of your pen. It resides in the hard drive of your computer. The story and stories you have been called to write exist already.

"Wait," I hear you say. "If they exist, why must I write them? If they exist, they have already been told. I'm done."

Would that it were that simple.

Those stories exist in another realm. The realm of dreams...the realm of fancy...another dimension somewhere beyond the three we know. Beyond the fourth of time as well. Somewhere beyond earth and sky, in that fantastical place where everything is possible, where miracles occur with each breath: That's where your story exists. In your heart: That's where your story exists. Encoded into every cell of your being: That's where your story exists.

Have you ever kept track of your dreams? If you have, you know how important it is to jot them down the moment you wake up. For if you don't, you're likely to forget them. It's the act of writing them down that gives substance to what is otherwise ethereal. It's the acting of carrying them from the kingdom of dreams into the physical reality of ink on a page that gives them substance, that allows you to connect with them. That allows them to touch you. That, in a real sense, makes them real.

So it is with your stories. They exist, just as your dreams do. But it's the act of setting them to the page, of letting one word follow the next and then the next and then the next, that makes them real, that "publishes" them.

That's right: The act of publishing is an act of making public. When you take your stories, those stories that have an existence only in your heart, an existence even your brain-mind may not see, when you take them and draw out the letters, stretch those letters into words and those words into sentences and paragraphs, magic happens. You take something that exists only in the airwaves, like a radio signal that broadcasts at a frequency not normally audible by the human ear, not normally picked up by even the most sophisticated audio equipment. You take that signal, which is your story, and translate it into a frequency that *is* audible. In doing that, you give it — and yourself — a new kind of life. A life in the public realm. A place on the radio dial of your life.

Perhaps you don't seek to have your work published in a conventional sense. Perhaps you do. At this moment, it doesn't matter. At this moment, all that matters is answering that call to write. All that matters is tuning in to that frequency, that normally inaudible signal, the one on which your Muse alone broadcasts, tuning in to it and taking down everything you hear. Everything. Without judgment. Without question. Without second-guessing. Without censoring.

Your Muse broadcasts to you on your private frequency. It is for you to tune in with the radio dial of your heart and transcribe.

No, you will not be "channeling." You will be cocreating — opening to the energy of your Muse, running it through the filters of your language and experience, and committing the resulting words, thoughts, ideas, scenes, poems, memories and songs to the printed page.

You are turning what already exists in the air around you (just as radio signals exist in the air around you) into something physical. Something you can touch. Something you can hold. Something you can read. In doing that, you are giving it a life it would not otherwise have.

If nothing happens beyond that, you will still have accomplished one of those breath-by-breath miracles I spoke of. Even if no one else sees or reads it, it has been published. It has been given a physical life it never had before. And just as every action in the universe has an impact on every being in that universe, or so our quantum scientists would have us believe, your words made manifest will have their effect.

If you do move from that point to print, that's a bonus. But that's not our starting point. Our starting point is you. You and your Muse. You and your stories. You and the word.

3.

The Muse Stream

I never know what's coming next...
That's why I go on, I suppose. To see what
the next sentence I write will be.

GORE VIDAL

No man ever steps in the same river twice,
for it's not the same river and
he's not the same man.

HERACLITUS

Just Start, and Trust Your Inner Vision

Just start, and trust your inner vision. Just start, and know that the words that long to pour from your heart will find their way onto the page — thought by thought, word by word, breath by breath. For the words are there. The story is there. It exists already — in another dimension, a parallel reality. It exists with a life and an imperative of its own.

Just start, and know the words will flow. Know they will flow without having to know what they are or where they will carry you when you free your story to unfold onto the page.

See the words appear as magically as the lemon-juice ink we used as children to create invisible writing. Hold your page to the light — the light of your heart and the light of your truth — and let your words take shape.

Watch the letters form on the page. See them combine into words, the words join into sentences, the sentences unite into paragraphs and the paragraphs flow from page to page to page until the story is done, until the work is complete and you, who started with nothing but a blank page and faith in the power of your inner vision, are amazed and awestruck by the power of your pen.

Thirteen Rules for Writing

1. There are no rules.

There is no right way. There is no wrong way. There is only *your* way.

2. Get out of your own way.

As you write — as part of an exercise, in your journal or on a directed project — the best way to stay connected with your Muse and the work at hand is to get out of your own way!

Remember that the writing experience need not be logical by any conventional or worldly standard, so let that part of yourself go. Ask any element of your being that is logical, analytical, critical, cynical, doubt-filled or judgmental to step aside for the duration of your projected writing time. By breathing into your heart and breathing out any fear, you will stay in the flow of inspiration and embark on a journey of infinite magic, wonder and awe.

Always align your mind to the wisdom of your heart. Open to the images that pour through you. Listen to the voice of your heart, your soul, your Muse. Let that voice guide you — as you write and as you live.

3. Leap into the void...and trust.

Trust that every word you are ready to write exists in the inkwell of your pen. Follow that pen wherever it takes you. Don't push your pen across the page. Surrender to it. Don't worry about being polite, appropriate or correct. Don't worry about making sense. Don't worry about anything. Just blurt it out. What seems silly in the moment is nearly always higher truth...or art.

3a. Listen...and always go with your first thoughts.

Write the first thing that comes into your head — whatever it is. Second thoughts and second-guessing arise from that part of your mind that is judgmental or censoring. Trust that what's coming to you is what calls out to be expressed. Allow it to be expressed. Trust it and surrender to it.

4. Surrender to the Muse Stream.

Allow your pen to keep flowing across the page and don't stop for any reason.

Don't stop to correct spelling or grammar or to grope for the right word. If you can't think of a word, leave a blank space or write *xxx*. If you don't like a word you've written, circle it and move on. (On the computer, capitalize, bold or underline it, whichever is quickest.) If English isn't your first language and you find yourself struggling for an English word or phrase, write it in your native language...or any language. Make up words if you must, but keep writing.

Writing on the Muse Stream prevents your mind from getting in the way of your heart and stops your personality mind from blocking your creativity. The time to hone and polish is later. Now is the time to write.

If you feel your center straying or your mind taking charge, return to your breath and focus on it (see #9). Your breath may also help you retrieve words and images from the deepest wells of your inner vision.

5. Be in the moment.

Be in the moment with each word...word by word. The word that trips off your fingers and onto the page or keyboard is the only one that matters. Were you to stop and think about each word, were you to stop and analyze, judge and left-brain each word, there would be no next word. Stay in the flow. Remember, the next word always comes...if you don't worry about it. If you let it.

6. Go for the jugular.

Go for *your* jugular. Go for the demon you would run from. Go for the feeling you would flee from. Go for that emotion you would deny. Once you put it on paper, you strip it of its power over you. Once you put it on paper, you free it to empower your work.

7. Love yourself and your words.

Treat your creation as an act of the heart. Love whatever issues from your pen without judgment. Be gentle with yourself. If you can't help but judge, wait an hour, a day, a week or a month before rereading or sharing what you have written. (See *Creative Support*, Chapter 14.)

8. Abandon all preconceptions.

Free yourself from all preconceptions regarding form, structure, content, audience or market. Don't force your words into a box. Don't fence them in. Let your words be in charge.

Start writing and discover all that you are, all that you desire, all that you feel, all that you touch and all that you know...and the perfect form will present itself.

9. If you get stuck...

Don't stop! Keep your pen moving. This alone will carry you through and past most fear and hesitation. Before you know it, you'll be back in a free and easy flow.

Here are five ways to keep your pen moving:

- *Repetition.* Repeat anything to keep your pen moving: the previous word or sentence, your starting word or sentence, or anything at all, even if it's "I don't know what to write" or "This is dumb" or "Why did I buy this book?" Don't judge the repeated words or phrases. Some may prove to be an integral part of the final work. You'll discard others in future drafts.

- *Free-association.* Let one word trigger the next — whatever leaps to mind, however silly. Let that word trigger the next, the next and so on...until the flow returns. (See *Why Aren't You Writing?*, page 45.)

- *Nonsense words.* Make up words...words that sound funny...words that sound weird...words that don't exist in any dictionary. Make one up, write it down...then another...then another...then another. This playful act tricks your inner censor into dropping its guard. Soon, nonsense words will become regular words and the flow will resume.

- *Breath.* The best way to remain present and in the flow is through your breath. Write "I am breathing in" as you inhale, "I am breathing out" as you exhale. Keep doing that until the flow returns. (See *The Breath of Creativity*, page 116.)

- *Doodles.* Draw or doodle. Do anything to keep ink flowing onto your page. Before long, squiggles will make way for words, words will form into sentences and you'll forget that you ever felt stuck.

10. Write.

Write and let the words flow from your pen onto the page. Write and let the spirit of who you are emerge onto the page. All those things will happen the moment you unlock the gates that have kept the words, ideas, thoughts and feelings dammed up inside you.

The Muse Stream frees you to allow that flow to happen. How? By training you to keep writing — through doubts, hesitation, fear and (seeming) unknowingness.

Here's how to get going:

- Settle into a physical, emotional and spiritual state of stillness. Use some of the rituals described in *Seven Tools for Transition* (page 142), if you need help.

- Keep the tips listed in #9 available for easy reference.

- Pick a starting word or phrase (I call them key words or phrases), either at random or from *Fifty Keys to Unlock Your Writing* (page 40). Or use *Finding Your Own Key* (page 39). If you're working on a particular project, use the last sentence you wrote before stopping as your key phrase or use *Finding Your Own Key* to find an alternative starting point.

- Set a timer for fifteen, twenty, thirty or sixty minutes. Place the face of the timer out of view and do not look at it while you're writing. (You will be amazed at how much you can write in fifteen or twenty minutes, as long as you stay in the Muse Stream.)

- Begin to write, opening with your key word or phrase. Then allow your pen or keyboard to carry you the rest of the way.

- Do not stop for any reason until the timer's alarm goes off. As you gain confidence with the process, a timer won't be necessary.

- If you get stuck, restore your flow by referring to the suggestions listed in *If You Get Stuck*.

- When you're done, do not read or share your writing until you can do so from an objective place of no-judgment. (See *After You've Written*, Chapter 13.)

11. Set easy goals.

If you're able to write only once a week, make that your goal and meet it. If you can set aside only ten minutes a month for writing, make that your goal and meet it. The easier your goals, the more likely you are to attain them. The more you do, the better you will feel about yourself and about writing. And the more you will write.

12. Empower yourself.

This is *your* creative journey. Don't let anyone else take charge of it.

Listen for the voice of your Muse as you leap, listen, surrender, trust and explore, as you rediscover the beauty and power of your words, your stories...your creativity.

13. There are no rules.

Even these rules aren't rules. They are guidelines that have worked for me and my students on many different kinds of writing projects. But they're not gospel. Play with them. Adapt them. Make them your own.

The Voice of the Muse Companion CD

I don't know about you, but when a book I'm reading includes guided meditations that it suggests I record and use, I hardly ever do it. Instead, I close one eye and read the meditation with the other, hoping it will have the desired effect.

It rarely does.

So, to do for you what I never get around to doing for myself — and to avoid being one of those authors who writes guided meditations that no one uses — I have created a two-CD recording of the ten major meditations in this book, including the *Meet Your Muse* meditation that follows on the next page. *The Voice of the Muse Companion CD* also includes a recording of the *Thirteen Rules for Writing* for those moments when you need a Muse Stream refresher or an inspirational boost.

You'll find order information at www.lightlinesmedia.com.

Meet Your Muse

Guided Meditation #1

For optimal results, record this guided meditation and play it back for your own use, or have a friend read it to you. A version recorded by the author is also available on The Voice of the Muse Companion CD *(see page 35).*

Relax. Close your eyes. Get into a comfortable position. Let your shoulders drop. And drop some more.

Take a few deep breaths, breathing in calm and quiet, breathing out fears, fatigue, stress. You're relaxed but alert. Awake and aware. Moving into a quiet place. A deep place. A place of creative freedom, creative vision, creative awakening.

In your mind's eye, see a door. A beautifully crafted door. Handcrafted. A work of art.

Perhaps it's a new door, newly discovered. Perhaps it's ancient, as old as time, just waiting for you to *re*discover it. See it or sense it...however you see it or sense it.

This is your doorway of inner vision. Walk up to it. Run your hand over it. Feel its texture...its richness...its depth.

As you touch the door, it swings open. The door to your inner vision will always swing open at your touch...if you let it.

You are the key.

Now the door swings open and you step across the threshold. Into a wondrous place. Perhaps you recognize this place. Perhaps it's new. Whatever you see or sense and however you see or sense it is perfect, perfect for you, in this moment.

See or sense this place, this wondrous place. See or sense it fully, using all your senses.

What does it look like? What colors do you see? How is the light? Do you hear any sounds? Smell any smells?

Reach out and touch something. Feel its texture.

What is the spirit of this place? What does it feel like, to you?

Now, coming toward you through this wondrous place, coming toward you bathed in light, is your Muse. Your creative spirit. The being that, in this moment, embodies your purest creative source, that font of creative energy, inspiration and revelation that we all have within us.

This is yours. Unique to you.

However it manifests, whatever you see, sense or feel of it, is right for you. In this moment.

Open your mind and heart. Allow it to come to you in whatever form it comes, recognizing that its form can change from moment to moment, mood to mood, writing project to writing project.

There is no right or wrong image, right or wrong way. There is only the way you see or sense, and what you see and sense. And it's perfect. For you.

What does your Muse look like? Feel like to you?

See or sense it fully. Again, use all your physical senses — sight, touch, smell, taste, sound. And your intuitive senses — feeling, spirit, essence.

Your Muse now stands before you, and you greet each other in whatever way feels right, taking all the time you need.

Now, you and your Muse begin a special dialogue.

Perhaps your Muse has a message for you. Perhaps you have questions for your Muse — questions about a specific project, questions about which is the right project for you right now, or general questions about your creative life.

Be open to whatever comes up. Let the dialogue go where it will.

Take thirty seconds of silence for this conversation. Transcribe it if that will assist you. If you choose to write at this time, pause the recording until you're done.

Now that you feel complete with that interaction, step forward. Take another step. Then another, moving closer and closer to your Muse...until you step into your Muse, until you and your Muse become one, merging in a wondrous moment of creative union.

What does that feel like? What sensations or emotions run through you? What do you see? Sense? Hear? Intuit?

Breathe deeply into the merged entity you are and experience all there is to experience...feel all there is to feel...be all there is to be.

Take twenty seconds of clock time to experience this fully.

Now that you feel complete, step back and away from your Muse. Note any feelings or sensations that action sparks for you. As you step away, thank your Muse for assisting you today and allow your Muse to respond.

Before you leave this place, your Muse hands you a gift, an expression of appreciation for having been freed into your life more consciously. What is it?

Receive this gift and keep it with you.

Recall it, if you choose, every time you sit down to write.

Now, turn back to the door — that special door — knowing that you can return to this place at any time to meet with your Muse. All you need to do is remember how it felt to be here. All it takes is stillness. A quiet time. A quiet place, where you're free to envision, where it's safe to create.

Once more, you touch the door, it swings open and you step through... and back.

As you return to your starting place, you bring back with you all that you sensed and all that you saw and all that you heard, felt and intuited. You're bringing it back to your conscious awareness, remembering whatever, in this moment, it serves you to remember.

When you're ready, but only then, open your eyes, staying with all you experienced.

Write about it — what you saw, felt or sensed. Write about the conversation you had with your Muse. Write whatever you remember, whatever comes up, taking all the time you need.

Remember to keep your pen moving across the page. Remember to breathe. Remember to censor nothing, freeing the voice of your Muse to live again through you on the page.

Finding Your Own Key

The word or phrase that launches your writing journey is the key that frees the voice of your Muse and unlocks the flow of your creativity. The particular word or phrase that comes to you through the following exercise or on your own is less important than the act of surrender it represents. And so when a key word or phrase emerges into conscious awareness, surrender to it — without censorship or judgment. Then let each succeeding word follow that one with the same freedom...until the last speck of ink is dry on your page.

Practice this brief meditative exercise until you can do it anywhere...at home... on a walk...in the car, bus or subway...in an airport terminal...on a plane.

Go within, into your inner spiritual and emotional space, eyes open or closed as desired or required by your situation.

Breathe deeply. In and out five, ten or fifteen times to a count of five, six or seven. Breathe into your connection with your Muse or whatever you choose to call your creative spirit.

Breathe out all fears, anxieties, worries. Breathe out your immediate surroundings and all distractions they could inject into your space.

Breathe yourself into a place of creation and connection, a place where you are one with your words, your writing, your project.

After your fifth or tenth breath, or whenever it happens, reach within... deep within. Reach within and let a word or phrase emerge. Don't judge it. Don't actively choose it. Let it emerge. Writing on the Muse Stream is always about letting and allowing. Let a word or phrase emerge from the depth of your being and allow it to bubble up to your conscious mind.

Allow yourself to hear it, to sense it, to know it. Then let it flit and flitter down to your fingers, to your pen or keyboard. Let it flow onto the page and allow yourself to flow from it. Without thinking. Without judging. Just being. Being that word, then the next and then the next.

Let the writing carry you on whatever journey of discovery the word or phrase sparks. The key word or phrase is your guide. Let it guide you, then, as you surrender to it and write.

Fifty Keys to Unlock Your Writing

Pick a word or phrase from the list on the next page. It doesn't matter which because when you surrender to the journey, the perfect words will always emerge, regardless of how you begin. Still, key words and phrases offer not only convenient starting points but are able to trick your logical, fearful or judgmental mind into abandoning control.

Choose your word or phrase using any of the following four methods and let it be the key to your next creative adventure:

- Pick a word or phrase at random.

- Close your eyes and let your finger drop to a word or phrase.

- Close your eyes, choose a number between one and fifty and let that number direct you to your key.

- Run through the list in order, one word or phrase per writing session.

Feel free to play with the list: Add your own words, alter the phrases, change tenses, turn positive statements into negatives or combine words and phrases. Creativity is about having fun...so have fun!

1. Red

2. I desire…

3. Green

4. If only…

5. I am a writer because…

6. I feel…

7. Purple

8. Sometimes, I wish…

9. Blueberries

10. My mother always told me to…

11. Bear

12. The smell of…reminds me of…

13. She turned and said, "…"

14. Yellow

15. The wind tasted like…

16. Eagle feathers

17. I don't feel…

18. I wish he had never…

19. Rabbit ears

20. I trust

21. When I was five…

22. Now that I'm five…

23. Tiger

24. When I looked into the ant hole, I saw…

25. Money

26. The earth sounded like…

27. Sex

28. I close my eyes and see…

29. I open my heart and know…

30. The curtain rose and…

31. "Lizards? What do you mean, lizards?"

32. The door slammed shut…

33. I desire…

34. My book (story) is about…

35. Leap

36. I love…

37. God

38. Hula hoop

39. I don't trust…

40. Muse

41. When I touched my tongue to the tree…

42. Creation

43. Word

44. She's lying…

45. The door opened…

46. Truth

47. I hate to write because…

48. I write to…

49. The end.

50. The beginning…

The Power of Your Pen

Pick up your pen and hold it in your hand. Feel its weight and texture. Study its form and aspect. Sense its potential.

Can you see or imagine the ink that sloshes around in the barrel as you move it this way and that? Can you visualize the waves that crash from one shore to the next — waves of blue or black or, if you're more fanciful in your implements, magenta or fuchsia?

Your words bob up and down in that sea of ink, in that ocean of story that ebbs and flows from barrel to nib to page.

Don't push your pen as you set it down on the pristine whiteness of the virginal page. Follow it. Allow it to carry you on a wondrous journey as you surrender to it and allow it to chart the course of your creativity.

Follow your pen. Let it guide you on a safari into the darkest of Amazon jungles, the uncharted territory of your deepest self.

Your pen will map out the journey, inking your itinerary as it forms before your eyes, allowing you and your readers the freshness of new experience.

Follow your pen, as I do at this moment, not knowing where it will carry me, allowing my terror to exist side-by-side with my awe and wonder, each word emerging despite my resistance to it.

I, too, fear the unknown, despair at the necessary surrender. I, too, long to know how this sentence will end and who I will be when it does.

I cannot know…need not know…at times dare not know.

All any of us can do who are called to this journey is place one word after the next and then another and then another, allowing the power of our pen — or of our fingers skipping across the keyboard — to chart the way, pen stroke by pen stroke, pixel by pixel, moment by moment, breath by breath.

Surrender to the Journey

In June 1997, I embarked on an odyssey whose consequences I could never have predicted...or imagined. I had been back living in Toronto for only a short while when a voice in my heart urged me to pack all I owned (not a lot) into the back of my Dodge Caravan and head west.

At other times in my life, I would have doubted the message, questioned my sanity. On that sunny morning, I knew my only choice was to trust and follow my heart.

For three months I journeyed. I traveled north and west from Toronto along the rugged, forested shores of Lake Huron and Lake Superior, then south and west, crossing Minnesota, North Dakota, South Dakota, Wyoming, Montana, Idaho and Oregon. From the Oregon coast, I slipped south into California, then shot back east, across Nevada and Utah, before dropping into northern Arizona.

Throughout those months, I never planned my next stop. When I tried, my plans were nearly always thwarted by some seemingly outside force. Mostly, I let my heart control the steering wheel and I followed wherever it took me.

It was a magically transformative experience, though not without stress, for it was difficult at times to surrender fully. Part of me longed to plot out an itinerary, to know where I would drive the next week, to know where I would end up. The greater, more courageous part of me trusted in the infinite wisdom of the journey.

Through all the unexpected stops, unanticipated detours and unpredicted forays into uncharted territory, all I could do was trust in each moment and believe that the story I was living would reveal itself — through the living of it.

It did — magnificently.

On the morning of the full moon in September, after ninety days of journeying, I drove into Sedona, Arizona. I expected this to be another whistle stop on the road to wherever. Instead, one week grew to two, one month to seven. Before I knew it, I had a new country, a new wife and a new baby on the way.

Had I given my brain-mind the control it sought, I might never have left Toronto, might never have launched a journey that gifted me with so much richness.

Part of what prepared me for this odyssey was *The MoonQuest*, the novel whose early drafts I had already written much as I lived that journey: moment by moment and word by word, ignorant of the outcome but trusting that one would emerge.

When we surrender to our heart-mind, trusting that the outcome will be more wondrous than anything we could consciously imagine, it always is.

As you write, let your pen carry you as my Dodge Caravan did me — in trust and surrender. Let it carry you to the story you didn't know you knew as, breath by breath, you move toward an outcome that has yet to reveal itself.

Here's a suggestion:

In today's writing, notice all the times your mind edges (or leaps) ahead of the word you're writing. Be aware as that controlling part of yourself reaches forward to find out what's coming next, where you're headed, how it will end. Notice when this happens, but don't judge or punish yourself. Simply return your focus to the word of the moment. Return to it gently, lovingly, reassuringly. And continue writing, in the moment, letter by letter and word by word.

Why Aren't You Writing?

Why aren't you writing? You don't know what to write? It doesn't matter. Write anyway. Place one word, any word, on the page. A single word. That's all it takes.

That single word, whatever it is, will launch you on a journey into your creativity and beyond your imagination. One word is all it takes. Open any book to a random page, close your eyes and point.

Write that word.

What about the next word, and the word after that? And the word after that? What about sentences and paragraphs? What about a subject?

You are the subject. I don't mean you will be writing about yourself — though you might be. You are the subject and your pen is sovereign. And that pen will carry you on an extraordinary journey of discovery, if you let it...writing flowingly and freely, letting the sentences unfold without your conscious mind getting in the way.

What you will experience is freedom *from* your mind, freedom for your heart, freedom of the story, freedom of the word.

When you write on the Muse Stream, you throw off the shackles of logic and leap into the inkwell of the unknown — a well within which reside all the stories you could ever want to write, all the catharsis you could ever want to experience, all the emotion you could ever want to express.

It's so simple.

Take the first word you write and, without thinking, write another. It needn't flow logically from the first. Perhaps it's an association — "chair" makes you think of "table." What does "table" remind you of? Don't think about it. Let the first word that comes to you, whatever it is, be the next word you write.

It doesn't make sense? It doesn't have to make sense. It may be better if it doesn't.

Just let one word trigger another and then another, until something shifts — and it will — and the flow is undammed.

Or perhaps "chair" reminds you of your first day in school or the old stuffed armchair you curled up in or hid behind as a child. Perhaps it triggers a story about that chair. About your childhood. Write it. Perhaps it triggers another story or emotion. Write it.

It triggers a blank? Write the same word again. And again. And again. Keep repeating it until something shifts, and you find yourself in a flow of words that carries you along with it. Don't fight the flow. Let it carry you on a current of words, images and emotions. Let it carry you across a new frontier and into a new land of wonder, joy and awe.

Pen v. Computer

The question I'm asked more than any other is whether I write longhand or on the computer. The answer? Both.

I wrote *The MoonQuest*'s first two drafts with pen and paper, but not because it was an objectively superior method. I wrote *The MoonQuest* by hand because I associated typing with too many years of freelance writing assignments, of expressing other people's ideas to the pressure of other people's deadlines.

Writing longhand helped me break old patterns and freed me to create in new ways. The heart-hand-paper connection is a powerful one and it supported my process.

My routine was to write longhand in the morning and input the day's writing in the evening, being careful to make no changes as I typed. If the temptation to edit was overpowering, I placed the desired change in square brackets so as not to lose the original — a good thing, as I returned to the original at least half the time.

By the time I composed this book, I had erased enough old conditioning to be able to move easily between pen and keyboard, writing longhand in the car and on the computer at home.

As I write *The StarQuest*, sequel to *The MoonQuest*, I'm largely on the computer — unless I'm feeling stuck, when I return to pen and ink and the potent union of heart, hand and paper.

You and Your Computer

One of the computer's greatest gifts can be its greatest curse: the ability to edit with ease. When you're writing anything on the Muse Stream, the last thing you need is the temptation to edit. Once you begin editing, you encourage your critical, censorious self to take command and shut off the flow.

There is a time to edit and revise, a time to correct and clarify. That time is later. Now is the time to write.

If your computer beeps at you over poor spelling or grammar, turn off the beep. If it underlines questionable words, switch off that feature as well. Disable any prompt that reminds you of anything that requires immediate correction.

If you can't resist the temptation to edit, judge or second-guess while writing, turn off your monitor or dim or cover your screen.

If blanking your screen is not possible, type with your eyes closed. But be sure your fingers are on the right keys (to avoid typing gibberish) and that you save frequently and back up your files (in case you mistakenly delete what you've written).

For help dodging other computer-related distractions, see *I Can't Write Until I...*, page 136.

You and Your Pen

The itch to edit as you write doesn't vanish when you turn off your computer. Even with pen and paper, it's easy to succumb to the impulse to cut, correct, reword and rework.

Once you step out of the Muse Stream to do that, it's even easier to fall back into the judgment and self-censorship that stunt your creativity.

To minimize this risk, try any or all of these when writing longhand:

- Write single-spaced with narrow margins that leave no room for alterations.

- Cross nothing out.

- Write with your eyes closed.

Here's a suggestion:

One advantage of pen-and-paper over the computer is that it frees you to approach your creativity more creatively. Let these ideas trigger your own:

- Break the "rules" by writing on unlined (unruled) paper or by turning ruled paper sideways and writing "against the rules." Write diagonally across the page. Write in spirals. Do anything to break established patterns.

- Reconnect with your playful child-self by writing with brightly colored felt-tip markers or writing on brightly colored paper. Switch colors partway through.

- Write with your non-dominant hand.

Abandon Control

Do you struggle? Perhaps you control too much and surrender too little.

Abandon control.

There can be no control in your writing, not if you choose to write from the heart. Control comes from a place of seeking safety where there is and cannot be any. Control comes from a place of armoring where there is and cannot be any.

There can be no control.

Period.

The moment you try to establish control is the moment the flow stops.

Cold.

Dead.

There can be no control or there is no flow. That may be the scariest concept in this book...in the universe, perhaps. But it is truth.

The moment you say "I can't say that," you shut something off. You shut something down. You turn off the tap and all that's left is the drip-drip-drip of a soul that yearns for expression but cannot find its way out.

Abandon control. Remove the word "control" from your emotional vocabulary. *There can be no control.* There is no simpler way to state it. There is no simpler concept that is more difficult to implement. *There can be no control.*

What about those who outline everything to the nth degree before they begin to write?

It doesn't matter what any writer or all writers are doing or not doing, what any teachers are saying or not saying (including this one), what any books are proposing or not proposing (including this one). Do what resonates for you...what feels right in your heart.

There are no rules...other than the rule that states that there are no rules. What works is what works best for you, in this moment. Something else may work better in the next. Therein lies the importance of being in the moment. In this moment. Being in any other is a doomed attempt at control.

My way need not be yours. For me, though, in this moment, my words, including these, are neither plotted nor planned. At this moment in my heart life and in my writing life, my words can only be surrendered to — fully, nakedly and honestly. That is where my healing lies.

Where does your healing lie?

Whenever we surrender to a higher imperative and abandon control, we are engaged in a healing act. Whenever we reach deep into our soul and allow *its* words to live through us, a healing occurs.

For me, my willingness to create more freely has helped me to live and love more fully — without the controls that have diminished me in the past. My healing lies in that expansion, in the unfettered creativity that inspires a life lived without limits.

Where does your healing lie? Write about it — freely and with no controls. Begin with "my healing lies" and continue, on the Muse Stream for ten minutes, twenty minutes if you can, thirty if you dare.

If you're writing on ruled paper, turn the page sideways and write "against the rules" to remind you to push past all that boxes you in, all that binds you to conformity, all that controls you. (See *You and Your Pen*, page 49.)

Creating Perfection

Are you frustrated? Do you struggle to find the perfect words that consummately evoke the depth of your passion or flawlessly paint the fullness of your vision? Are you frustrated because the words you have chosen seem inadequate, their ordering unsatisfactory?

You're not alone. Many writers would echo your frustration.

It's a futile frustration, for language is an approximation. It's a powerful but often inadequate device for translating experience and emotion into a form others can share.

As I write these words, the sun is sliding through a marbled Hawaii sky toward the Pacific, its light skipping across wind-rippled waters.

If I have been successful in my description, you will see some version of an ocean sunset. Some version, but not mine.

It may approach mine. It may approximate mine. Yet my words, as expertly as I may have deployed them, cannot create a Kodak moment. (Even Kodak can't create a perfect Kodak moment.) My words are more likely to create an Impressionist moment.

That is not a bad thing. It gives readers space to have their own experience, to paint their own pictures from the words you have freed from your pen.

Just as you cannot control the words that flow from you, you cannot control your reader's experience of those words. Nor would you want to. How often have you been disappointed by a film portrayal of your favorite literary character because your inner director cast the role more astutely than the movie director did?

Empower your readers to have their own experience and recognize that all you can do is translate your experience as heartfully as you're able into little squiggles on a page. Begin by recognizing that most of the time you're only going to come close. Continue by knowing that it remains within your power to have your words incite revolution, topple dynasties, overthrow "reality."

That's perfect enough for me. How about you?

Here's a suggestion:

What are you waiting for? Pick up your pen. Describe what you see, what you feel, what you yearn for, what you love. Don't try to be perfect. Don't try at all. Just allow. And know that from that place of surrender, you are creating perfection.

Trust. Let Go. Leap.

When you sit down at the blank page or screen, you have three simple tasks:

Trust.

Let go.

Leap.

Trust.

Trust that each word that emerges is the correct and appropriate one. Don't judge.

Trust your imagination.

Trust past your imagination, which has its own limits, and trust those creative sources that guide and inspire you.

Trust the unknown.

Trust the depths of a passion you may not even know you feel.

Trust the light that kindles your faith — your faith that one word will lead to the next, that two words will form a cogent and coherent thought, that each sentence will form part of a whole that is not visible in the writing of it.

It's easy to get so caught up in the word of the moment, the word that doesn't seem right or doesn't seem to make sense, that you cannot see the whole. Of course you cannot, for the whole has not yet come into its wholeness.

Let the words tell their story, your story. Then wait until the story is done to discern (not judge) where the meaning lies.

Trust each writing situation — as you trust each living situation — to be in your highest good. And it will be. In time you will see the underlying wisdom of your words and will come to recognize the wisdom in your life.

Let go.

Let go of any expectation whatsoever, including the one that states that what you write today will have any value beyond today, that it will serve or aid or heal or pay, that it is anything but what it is on the page.

No expectations.

None.

Of anything.

At all.

Period.

Let go of all preconceptions of form. Don't put your words into the straitjacket of a predetermined form. Your words will find their own shape and form. Your words will find their own place on the page, in the order and structure that suits them first and you second. You cannot always know that shape and form in advance.

Follow your fingers as they dance across your keyboard. Follow your words as they create the form that best suits your material, the structure that best suits your message, the message that best suits your readers.

No, this may not be the way other writing books tell you to write, particularly nonfiction. Outline, outline, outline, they say. There is a place for the outline. That place is not here, not now.

Sit down at the blank screen or blank page and let emerge what longs to emerge: those thoughts, ideas and miscellaneous strands that seem not to link with anything else. They do, even if the patterns elude you. The grand design will emerge...in the emerging of it.

Leap.

Leap onto that blank page and let your whole body fill it with its juices. You in your entirety. Your body. Your mind. Your soul. Your spirit. Your divinity.

Yes, your divinity. For every word you pen is an expression of that divinity. Your divinity is what links you with God, Buddha or the Christ-mind or whatever higher power you believe in. If you believe in none, than your deepest, heartfelt truth will be the fuel that fires your passion. For they are one and the same.

Leap onto the page with that first word, that first godlike piece of creation. Then leap from that word into the next and into the next and into the next. And into the next.

Leap off one cliff and then off another and then off another. And know that you are safe. There is no splat onto the ground. Even if there were, it wouldn't matter. What matters is the word. The one word and then the next.

Keep writing and keep trusting that each word *will* lead to the next and the next and the next. For as long as you trust that it will, then it will. That's one thing I can guarantee. The words will always flow when you allow them to flow, when you surrender to them, fully...when you trust, let go and leap.

Now Is the Time to Write / I

This is a first draft that you write in this moment. This is an opportunity to release your Muse onto the page using the language of your heart, which may not yet be the perfectly executed language of your perfectly spelled, punctuated and grammared brain. That's okay. Allow it to be okay.

You can choose later to return to this draft and revisit it, review it, revise it — using your heart-mind to bring it into closer alignment with your heart-vision. That time will come (see *The Heartful Art of re-Vision*, page 203).

Now is the time to write, to let your Muse speak...to let your heart speak. Do that now and it will be good enough. It will be better than good enough. It will be yours.

Being yours, it cannot be told by anyone else.

Let's you and I and a dozen of our friends sit in the same field for a spell and watch the wind, smell the clouds and listen to the flowers. Though we will have shared a common experience, we will each create of it a different story.

Only you can tell your story. Only you can write your book. Only your story and your book will be infused with the uniqueness of your spirit, your outlook, your history and your heart. And infused as it will be with all those elements that both distinguish you from others and link you to all humankind, your story, poem, article or book will be as no other has been, is or ever will be.

Leave judgment to judges who sit on the bench. Leave analysis to the analysts. Leave criticism to the critics. Your mission this day is to write, to allow words to spill from you unhindered by judgment, unhampered by not-good-enoughs, uncrippled by comparisons. There is a time to write and a time to polish.

Now is the time to write.

Now is the time to write.

Now is the time to write.

Here's a suggestion:

Write. Now.

Write anything at all.

Write for five minutes or fifty but write, doing your best to leave judgment to the judges.

Write.

Now.

4.

Suspend Judgment

*Literature is strewn with the wreckage of men
who have minded beyond reason
the opinions of others.*

VIRGINIA WOOLF

*Our deepest fear is not that we are inadequate.
Our deepest fear is that we are powerful
beyond measure.*

MARIANNE WILLIAMSON

Keep Writing

You question as you write. I hear you.

Let the questions go. Let the doubts go.

What you write isn't the final draft and need not bear that ultimate perfection. It is perfect in this moment. For it is in this moment that you write it. And in this moment it is all that it needs to be: the perfect expression of who you are and what you are called to write, share and communicate out into the world.

You question the form your words are taking? Or the lack of form? You judge their structure or perceived lack of polish? Continue to let the words flow. Don't let your questioning get in the way of the writing. Know that form, structure and refinement will follow, will reveal themselves. For now, let your words determine their own shape.

Do not judge those words. Do not judge them any more than you would want to be judged. Have compassion for them. Forgive them for the places they have taken you that you were reluctant to visit. Forgive yourself for the thoughts and feelings you expressed through them that, until now, you didn't dare express. They are yours. Own them and move on to greater, freer writing, more powerful writing and with it, a greater, freer and more empowered life.

Suspend judgment. Keep writing through the judgment, until you're past the judgment. For only from a place of no-judgment can the true art and true heart expose itself — first to you and then to the world.

Keep writing. Don't punish yourself for your judgment, for then you are judging the judging, which is no healthier than judging anything else.

You feel judgment coming on? Acknowledge it. Write it. "I'm judging." Or "This isn't very good." Or "This is first-class, irredeemable crap." Say it and be done with it. And move on.

Do not stop.

Do not stop for any reason. Do not stop unless you must evacuate your house. Do not stop unless fire threatens to engulf your writing room.

Keep writing.

All those distractions that now tempt you have been created by that part of you that would prefer you not to be writing, certainly not to be writing whatever it is you're writing, which is somehow threatening whatever it is it's threatening. No. No, no and no. Keep writing.

Let the words flow. Without cease. They will if you will let them. They will if you trust.

Here's a suggestion:

It's the simplest of suggestions and the only one worth making: Write. Now!

Start any way. Write for any length of time about anything at all.

Just do it. Write. And keep writing.

Here's another suggestion:

There are many creative ways to arrive at your own key word or phrase. Here's a workshop favorite that's far more powerful than it first appears. All that's required is a single, blank sheet of unlined paper, a couple of colored pencils, markers or crayons and, of course, writing paper.

Holding one or two of the markers in one hand, close your eyes and begin to draw on the unlined paper. Don't peek, just draw, doodle or make whatever markings you're called to make. Keep at it for ten to twenty seconds, without lifting your pen(s) from the page.

When you're done, open your eyes, breathe deeply and, without judgment, look at your drawing without trying to analyze it. Continue to breathe and let one, two or three words or phrases bubble up into consciousness, triggered by your drawing. Don't judge or censor what emerges, no matter what it is.

As these words or phrases come to you, jot them down on your writing or drawing paper with one of your markers.

Using the word or phrase that has the most power for you, begin to write on the Muse Stream — with a colored marker if you prefer. Write for ten, twenty or thirty minutes. If you had more than one key word or phrase, write again using the next most powerful word or phrase.

Remember to always keep your pen moving. If you can't, see *If You Get Stuck*, page 32.

In This Moment

"What's the point?" you ask. "I don't know what to write that I haven't written a million times before."

Then write it a million and first time.

It doesn't matter how many times you write it. You are being called to write, to keep your pen moving across that page, to keep your fingers skipping over those keys. *What* you write matters not at all.

What matters in this moment is that you honor the imperative. What matters, again and again and again, is that words are forming before your eyes and that you are not planning those words. You are letting them emerge one at a time, in whatever sequence or jumble or nonsense they need to.

Not every day will produce a perfect chapter or scene or installment or poem. Many days will and many will not. Again, it matters not.

What matters is your engagement. What matters is your commitment. What matters is your will.

If you are allowing one word to follow the next with minimal conscious input then you are doing all that needs doing at this moment. This is not an exercise in utility. It's an exercise in flow, in allowing, in surrender. It's an exercise in retaining and maintaining your connection with your Muse.

Know that whatever you write is perfect. Know that whatever you experience is perfect. Know that whatever you feel is perfect.

Some days the temptation will be to regard each word that crosses your page with distaste, to view each sentence as a cruel mockery of the vision that first impelled you to the page.

Don't judge what you've written. Judgment day is another day. Today is a writing day. This is a writing moment.

Too often we sit in judgment of ourselves and our work from a place of fear and self-loathing. "This is not good enough," we think. "This will never be good enough." Or, "This story has been told better before by someone else." Or, "This book has been written before."

Know this now and for all time: It *is* good enough. In this moment, this word is good enough, and so is this one.

This moment is always as good as it gets — in this moment. So make the best of it. In this moment, give yourself permission to write the worst junk in the world, the same permission I give myself in this moment when I fear what I write for you isn't good enough. It is, in this moment. I must believe this, as must you, or we can never move into the next moment and then the next, when those moments, too, form the present moment.

It *is* good enough. If you do your best to write freely and easily from your heart, it is always better than good enough. It is perfect — in this moment, which is the only moment that matters, for it is the only moment that exists.

Let Judgment Go, and Let the Muse Stream Flow

Guided Meditation #2

For optimal results, record this guided meditation and play it back for your own use, or have a friend read it to you. A version recorded by the author is also available on The Voice of the Muse Companion CD *(see page 35).*

Breathe. Breathe in the quiet, white light of your creative essence, your divine essence, your Muse. Breathe in your fire, your flame, your beingness, your God-self. Breathe in the light of who you are, the truth of who you are, the love of who you are.

Breathe in all the light and aloha you are.

Aloha is not just a word that conjures up the gentle swaying of palm trees and hula dancers. Aloha is a consciousness, a state of being, a state of open-heartedness, a state of love in its truest, fullest sense.

Breathe into that openness within you. Breathe it in fully, deeply, completely.

Breathe out any doubts, any fears that you're not good enough, that someone else or anyone else — your friend who has already been published, your neighbor who writes better description than you do — is a more accomplished creator.

Breathe that out, for it is not true.

You are creative. You are innately creative. You are inherently creative. Everyone is. And because you are, you can express that creativity through writing, through placing one word after the next on the written page.

Let go of all feelings that you're not good enough. For you are.

Release all feelings that others are better than you. They are not.

You are equal to all and equal to the joyful task at hand, which is expressing the words and passions of your heart in written form.

You are equal to it, for you were born to it. Every micro-bit, every nano-bit of your being — physical, emotional and spiritual — has been encoded with that will, desire and aptitude to create.

You may lack certain skills. Those skills can be learned and practiced. In this moment, skills don't matter nearly as much as heart, intent and choice. You have the former. We all do. And you can tap into the latter two with ease.

Know that and be that.

It's simple. It's simple yet complex, for you are pushing against what may seem like lifetimes of programming.

What has been programmed can be erased — more quickly than the time it took to program into you.

You are good enough. You are better than good enough.

Despite what anyone ever said, despite any way in which you were treated — words and actions your conscious mind may have long ago forgotten or buried — despite any or all of these, you are a writer.

You *are* good enough. Your words are good enough. Your creations are good enough. Better than good enough. For they are the unique expressions of a unique heart that is, even now, opening to the prospect and possibility of finally being free to speak.

Feel that freedom. Open to that freedom. Embrace that freedom. It needn't frighten you. It needn't close you down. It is safe. For in that freedom lies all the truth of the universe, just as within you lies all the truth of the universe.

So put pen to paper, let fingers dance upon the keyboard and simply begin.

Begin at the beginning.

Let that first word be the God of the Old Testament, who allowed the world to form. "Let there be light," God said. Not, "I order and command light." Not, "The light must look a certain way, must be a certain brightness."

Creation is an act of allowing, of letting. *Let* there be light. *Let* there be creation. *Let* there be one story, and then another. And let the words that best express that story find their own way onto the page, without any need by you to intervene or get in the way.

Let.

Let the words be.

Let yourself be.

There is no judging in the act of letting. There is no call to judge. There is no call to take any active role whatsoever. Surrender to creation and let it be.

God didn't say as the earth formed, "You know, I don't like this island over here and that mountain over there." God allowed the earth to form and saw it, and it was good. God didn't judge it to be good. By allowing, it *was* good. Inherently good.

Allow your creations to form without judgment, and they, too, will be good.

Give your creations life. Then give them the free will to form as they will, to live their imperative.

Let.

Let them form.

Let them be.

Let them love you.

Let yourself love them back.

There is no need to judge. There is never any need to judge.

Let the words flow, and let judgment go. Let it fly...far, far away where it can do no more damage or harm to you or your words or your work. Or to anyone or anything.

Now, pick a word, any word.

Let a word or phrase bubble up into your consciousness. A word that expresses your state of beingness in this moment.

Don't judge it. Never judge.

Don't censor it. Never censor.

Allow.

Simply allow.

And when that word or phrase has emerged, let that be your starting point, your launching pad, your rocket, propelling you to the farthest reaches of the universe in a free-flowing flight of creation.

And so, write. Right now.

Remember to keep your pen moving across the page. Remember to *let* it move across the page. Free it and it will free you.

Let it fly and let yourself fly with it.

If you feel stuck, just keep going. Repeat. Free-associate. Write nonsense. Breathe. Doodle. Any or all of these will release the stuckness and propel you forward.

Write for as long as you can, until you feel complete...and then for a little bit longer if that feels right.

Write. Now.

Heartful Acts of Revolution

Perhaps you *will* be judged for what you write. Not everyone's heart is as open as yours, perhaps. But everyone's sings the same song.

Thus, the fiercest ridicule and loudest judgment will come from those who are touched most deeply by your words. That's right. The fiercest ridicule and loudest, cruelest judgment will come from those who are touched most deeply by your words. Let me say that one more time, for it is a radical thought: *The fiercest ridicule and loudest, cruelest judgment will come from those who are touched most deeply by your words.*

How is that possible? It's simple. Your critics are touched at a place deeper than they feel comfortable going, so their reaction and response is one of cruelty.

Their cruelty is not directed at you, though their minds and yours might think that. Their cruelty is directed toward themselves. It is themselves they would judge but cannot, dare not. So they direct their judgment outward, toward you.

Let it roll off you. Let it not matter. For it does not. No word that anyone can say to you — be it in love or fear — can or should alter the truth of your heart. Nor should it alter the truth of your path.

Walk gently on that path but speak — and write — from a place of strength.

Your most potent place of strength is your heart.

Your heart is in touch with everyone and everything that is, was or ever will be. Your heart knows all.

That is why it is so important to listen to your heart and trust in its truth. For all the truth that is, was or ever will be resides there. And as you touch that place, as you feel that place, as you are that place, your words will fill hearts, topple kingdoms and make whole what has been ripped apart — wherever they are read, whispered or sung.

That is the power of your heart. That is the power of your words.

Write from your heart. Write from your heart with courage and love.

Write from your heart as though nothing else mattered, and your words will be acts of revolution that transform worlds.

If you can't touch that place fully this time, you will touch it more fully next time and more fully still the time after that.

For there may be walls upon walls upon walls, topped with barbed wire and broken glass and guarded by monsters, demons and trolls, that encircle your heart. They may have been built up over years, over decades.

These walls have no power.

They can collapse in an instant. And in that same instant, all those monsters will turn out to be as tame and as loving as kittens...if you show them that there is no need to be cruel.

Everything is already there, already in place. All the stories, all the poems, all the healings, all the words are there, in the right order. Just tune that radio dial to K-HEART, the frequency of aloha, and all you require will appear without delay.

For there is no time. There is only now, only this word...and now this one... and now this one.

Then, before you know it you're done and kingdoms have toppled, demons are licking your face and the world has changed, for you have changed.

And next time, it will be easier.

Here's a suggestion:

Now, right now, commit an act of revolution. Write. Write anything, but write it from your heart. Write it from your heart, without judgment. And know that nothing will ever be the same again.

Taming Your Critic

Guided Meditation #3

For optimal results, record this guided meditation and play it back for your own use, or have a friend read it to you. A version recorded by the author is also available on The Voice of the Muse Companion CD *(see page 35).*

Sit or lie down in a comfortable position. Close your eyes and take a few deep breaths. Let yourself relax. Feel yourself relax on your breath.

Now, let your shoulders drop...and drop some more. And some more. And some more. Breathe deeply and fully, feeling the breath fill not only your lungs and abdomen but your entire body — from head to toes and back again.

And again.

And again.

Feel the breath cleanse you. Feel it dissolve your fears, your anxiety, your stress. Feel it strengthen you, empower you. Feel it protect you, keep you safe. Feel it open your heart. Feel it open your mind.

There have been times in your life when you have been criticized, times in your life when you have been judged. Of course there have. We've all had those experiences. As children. As adolescents. As adults.

Sometimes, the experience rolled off us painlessly. Sometimes, it felt excruciatingly cruel. Sometimes, we forged ahead in spite of it. Sometimes, it shut us down.

It's all normal, all perfect, all part of the human experience. And, as with all human experience, we can choose how to react or respond, we can choose how each instance will affect us.

Don't judge how you've reacted or responded in the past. Simply be aware and keep breathing. Fully. Deeply. Allow your breath to once again dissolve any stress or anxiety triggered by unpleasant memories.

Know that you are safe. Protected. Free from harm of any sort.

From that place of relaxed breathing, from that place of safety, call into your mind, heart and/or consciousness your harshest critic. Perhaps it's someone in your past or present life. A teacher. A parent. A sibling. Another relative. A friend. A school or neighborhood bully. A boss, professional colleague or coworker.

Feel whatever charge you feel around this individual, and breathe. Feel whatever charge you feel around this individual and let that feeling dissolve on your breath.

Now, let that critic transform into some kind of image, something that represents that critic, that stands in for that critic. A symbol. A metaphor. Perhaps it's an animal. Perhaps it's a color or shape. Perhaps it's a snake or serpent. Perhaps it's another human form or another type of form altogether. Or perhaps it doesn't change form at all.

Let it be what it is and know that however it shows up is perfect for you in this moment. Regardless of how it shows up, see it not as an external critic but as an internalized aspect of you, ready to engage with you.

Whatever it is, whoever it is, however it is, greet it and begin a dialogue with it. Have a conversation with it. Engage with it.

Either write this dialogue as it occurs or let it emerge silently in your heart.

In the first part of your conversation, ask your critic why it judged you so cruelly, what provoked its behavior, what it was afraid of.

If this is an ongoing situation, frame your questions in the present tense.

Listen with an open heart. Respond with an open heart. Allow compassion. Allow understanding. Allow forgiveness. Allow love.

Give yourself thirty seconds of clock time for this part of the experience. Or pause the recording until you are ready to continue.

Be aware that if you're experiencing judgment, there are probably areas in your life where you're expressing judgment. Have compassion for yourself for your judgments. Be understanding. Be forgiving. Be loving. Be open. Be respectful. Toward yourself.

Commit, as well, to directing those same attitudes toward others, toward anyone you are tempted to criticize harshly.

Now, as you return to the conversation with your critic, ask it how the two of you can work together from this moment forward to bring your work, your writing and your life to its fullest, most magnificent potential.

Converse. Discuss. Negotiate. Dialogue. Engage. Silently or in writing.

Again, be loving and compassionate. Be understanding and forgiving. Be respectful. Be open.

Allow another thirty seconds of clock time for this part of the experience. Or, again, pause the recording until you're ready to continue.

Now it's time to bring your encounter to a close. Thank this aspect of yourself for its assistance, for its openness, for its willingness to transform. And commit to this new partnership. Commit, too, to the spirit of cooperation the two of you have just forged in love and mutual respect.

When you're done, write of your experiences and discoveries. Use all your senses to paint a picture in words of your new awareness and your renewed creative power.

When you're finished writing, remember to read your words from a place of love, openness and nonjudgment. Remember, too, your commitment to partnership and cooperation.

5.

Listen to Your Heart

The eyes are blind.
One must look with the heart...

ANTOINE DE SAINT-EXUPÉRY

I cannot possibly tell you how I came to write
A Wrinkle in Time. *It was simply a book*
I had to write. I had no choice.

MADELEINE L'ENGLE

Listen

The art of writing is the act of listening. Only listening. That's all there is. Learn to listen to the voice of your heart, for it alone carries the stories, poems and truths that yearn to be birthed through you. You do not make anything up as you write on the Muse Stream. You are listening to *your* words and trusting that whatever you hear is whatever it is that calls to be recorded in this moment.

Perhaps in the next moment you will discern that those particular words have no place in this work. So be it. That is in the next moment.

In this moment, your job is to listen. Only listen. To be still enough that you can listen. To be still enough that you can hear the voice of your Muse, which holds the full repository of every story you have ever written or will write.

Be still. Begin from a place of inner stillness. Begin from a place of nothing but breath. In that stillness you will find the connection with your heart. Through that stillness you will hear the voice of your Muse.

Whenever that connection is threatened, whenever you cannot hear the voice of your Muse fully or clearly, return to the inner silence and refocus on your breath. Through your breath you can connect, listen and write under any circumstances, in any situation.

Be still and keep breathing.

Be still and trust.

Be still and listen.

Listen. Just listen. From listening you will know what to write and when to write it. You will know when to start and when to stop. You will know the form and the shape. You will know all you need to know. For all you need to know already resides in your heart.

You say that your heart has steered you wrong? That is not possible — not on the page and not in life.

You don't believe me? Consider first that it might not have been your heart that was speaking. Perhaps it was your brain. Or your stomach. Or another part of your body masquerading as your heart.

That's where discernment comes in. With discernment, you *know* whether it is right. You know if the word is right, if the topic is right, if the form is right. You know it in your gut. You know it in your soul. You know it in your heart.

Consider, also, this possibility: Your heart spoke, but you didn't like what you heard. So you ignored it. Or you ignored part of it. Or you heeded it and didn't like the outcome, not stepping back to see the bigger picture.

In that bigger picture, everything you write serves your highest good. That's not always easy to see in the moment. And the moment is not the time to make that determination. The moment is the time to be in the moment. Leave the rest to other moments...when they come.

Write now. And trust. Yes, outcomes might not be those your personality mind or child-self would prefer. They are not in charge. They cannot be if you are to live and write your authentic truth. For that truth resides only in the heart.

You fear the truth? That's a different matter.

"The truth shall make you free," Jesus said in a statement that speaks to all faiths and traditions.

Well, we don't always want the truth because we don't always want to be free. We like to think we're free without having to act free and take responsibility for that freedom. The true adult-self, living from the heart, experiences the freedom that flows from truth and takes responsibility for it.

What, you ask, has this to do with writing?

As in life, so in writing. If you already follow a spiritual path, apply all the precepts of your spirituality to your writing and you will need no writing instruction — from me or anyone else.

Live in the moment. Let the truth set you free. Surrender — to God, Buddha, Allah, Spirit or your Muse. Surrender to the higher power that is not truly outside of you, the higher power that resides within you. That is where your creative source resides. That is where you will hear the still, small voice that speaks the truth, your truth. That is the voice and truth you seek when you sit still and listen, when you connect and when, without censoring or questioning, you write what you hear.

All right, go ahead and question. It's healthy to question. But don't question while you're writing. Write what longs to emerge, however you may mistrust it in the moment. Just as I mistrust some of what I write here in this moment. Allow the words to emerge. Get them onto the page. Only then, and perhaps only after a suitable period of time has elapsed, is it appropriate to ask questions of them.

Too often, questions come from that part of ourselves that would prefer to avoid the truth at all costs. It's too fearful, too life-changing.

Art is life-changing. And the change begins with the artist. You write to discover who you are, to rediscover and remember the truth of who you are. In that rediscovery and remembering, you inspire others to do likewise.

Remember: Once your words are on paper, they already have a quantum effect on the world, whether or not they are shared or conventionally published. Once they are on paper, they have already changed *you*. And thus changed, you can't help but change the world.

So, listen. Listen through the silence to the rhythm of your heart, the voice of your Muse. Listen for a word, any word. Then dip your pen into the inkwell of your truth, touch it to the page and allow your words to set you free.

Heart Words

Heart words are filled with pain as well as joy, anger as well as love, fear as well as courage. Heart words are feeling words. Those are the words you are called on to engage. For only from your feelings can anything true be engaged.

Breathe now. Breathe in deeply. Breathe in deeply so that the twinges of panic or cynicism, of disbelief or mistrust, can be washed away with your out-breath. Breathe into your heart space, your heart center. Breathe into it and know that that's where the only reality worth writing about resides and from which the only source worth mentioning can be released.

You doubt? Of course you doubt. You have been closed down for so long, perhaps, writing dry words that have only safety to commend them.

There is no safety. I'll say it again: There is no safety. There is only a *perception* of safety.

That's the place I wrote from for many years, including nearly two decades as a freelance writer, writing from every place but my heart.

My words were chosen well. My technique was excellent. My grammar and spelling were faultless. Yet there were few words that could cause the tiniest twinge of recognition in my readers.

I reported what was outside without referencing it to what was inside. That felt safe. But the only safety was in the belief that no one would attack me for my words.

Yet no one would love me for my words, either. No one would feel connected to my words. My words never made anyone laugh or cry, never made anyone remember their joys or pains, never connected my truth to theirs. It was a veneer, like a suit of armor, that kept me separate.

There is no separateness. Every heart word we write has the potential to change someone, touch someone, heal someone, open someone's heart — through laughter or tears, through memories or fantasies, through the truth that is only expressed through emotion, which is only expressed through the heart.

Write from the Heart

Guided Meditation #4

For optimal results, record this guided meditation and play it back for your own use, or have a friend read it to you. A version recorded by the author is also available on The Voice of the Muse Companion CD *(see page 35).*

Relax. Close your eyes. Focus on your breath. Breathe deeply. In and out. In and out. In and out. Continue to breathe, in and out, breathing in relaxation, breathing in freedom...allowing any stress, anxiety or tightness to relax into freedom on your breath.

Listen to the rhythm of your heart. Feel it beating. Feel it pumping life throughout your body. Down into your abdomen, groin, legs, feet and toes. Up into your neck and shoulders, your mouth, nose and ears, your eyes. Feel its power in your arms, hands and fingers. The hands you write with. The hands of creation.

Feel that life force circulate freely, spiraling throughout your body, creating patterns and shapes, colors and sounds. Listen to the rhythm of that life force that is centered in your heart. And in that rhythm, through that rhythm, listen for the voice of your Muse.

What does it mean to write from the heart? Is it physically possible? Can your fingers reach back in on themselves, travel up your arms, past your elbows and shoulders, then down your chest to touch that central mind that, were it truly in charge, would revolutionize your writing and your life?

For, yes, your heart is your central mind — a mind more powerful, life-fulfilling and life-affirming than your brain, as powerful and magical a piece of machinery as that is. But that's what it is: a piece of machinery. A wondrous, miraculous machine, but a machine nonetheless.

When we let machines do our writing for us, when we let machines do our living for us, the result is mechanical, soulless and spiritless.

We don't touch others at a deep level when we connect mind-to-mind, though that connection is a powerful and important one. We touch others at a deep level when we connect heart-to-heart.

So, let your fingers reach back in on themselves. See them traveling through your arms...on the inside not the outside.

See them reaching past your wrists and up your forearms, past your elbows and up to your shoulders. Let them stop there for a moment and, from their place deep inside your muscles, bone and tissue, massage and caress the tension from in and around those shoulders.

Feel the release as your fingers press deeply into the soul of your shoulder, releasing all the stress, all the fear, all the tightness, all the anxiety, all the "shoulds."

Notice the word "should." See it write itself out in your mind's eye and see that this word "should" forms seventy-five percent of the word "shoulder."

It's in our shoulders that we hold all our shoulds. And it's from our shoulders that our shoulds must be released.

Now is the time to massage those shoulds away. Now is the time to un-should-er and feel the lightness return to your shoulders, to your entire body.

Now is the time to let the burden drop from your shoulders. Now is the time to unshoulder all you have been bearing. All the responsibility. All the weight. All the burdens of this time and all time.

Feel your fingers massage them away...out of your shoulders and out of your neck. Let the shoulds dissolve: "I should write about this"; "I should write this way"; "I should be careful not to offend"; "I should be doing this or that instead of writing"; "I should be writing instead of doing this or that."

Let those shoulds and all shoulds melt under your touch. Let that sense of lightness and freedom you were born with begin to return, even if only for a moment.

Once you feel the return of some of your natural lightness, once you feel some of that un-should-ering, let your fingers continue down to your heart — both the organ at the left side of your chest and the chakra or energy center in the middle of your chest.

Let your fingers continue down, and as they do, let them clear away any cobwebs, let them unlock any doors, gates or walls, let them move in gently and caress that place of love with love.

Let the energy of that love, that aloha, of that place of heart-centered-ness, fill your fingertips.

Let the memory of all the love you have experienced, all the loving experiences you have lived, let that memory fill your fingertips so that when, in a few moments, you return them to the keyboard or pen, that love will infuse every letter and word that flows from them, from that connection to your heart that is always there and can always be reignited.

Continue to breathe, to breathe deeply, as you open your heart and clear away and free all that has been scarred, barricaded and bottled up.

Breathe in the clarity. Breathe in the focus. Breathe in the love, the self-love, the love of your heart, your Muse, your words. Breathe in the aloha.

Continue to breathe, in and out, in and out, for a few more moments.

In and out.

In and out.

In and out.

Slowly.

Deeply.

Fully.

As you breathe, listen. Focus your attention on your heart. Focus all your attention on your heart. In this moment, let nothing exist but your heart.

Listen to it. Listen for its voice, for the voice of your Muse as expressed through your heart. Listen to your heart. Still yourself and listen.

Your heart has a message for you. A word, a phrase...many words, many phrases. As you continue to focus and listen, you will hear it. Clearly.

Once you begin to hear it, begin to write what you hear.

Continue listening and writing, listening and writing, recording all that you hear or sense, in this moment.

And now this one.

And now this one.

If you hear or sense nothing at this time, don't judge yourself. Simply launch your journey using this key phrase: "My heart speaks to me of..."

In either case, write on the Muse Stream, remembering to keep your pen moving across the page, letting it be the medium through which your heart words speak to you.

Write your heart words until you sense completion.

Then hold the silence for a few moments longer...open to anything new your heart has to say.

Write What You Know...If You Dare

Write what you know. How often have you heard that? How often has it frustrated you?

"I can't write about a black man unless I'm black."

"I can't write about a woman unless I'm a woman."

"I can't write about flying an airplane unless I'm a pilot."

"I can't write about a gay man or a lesbian because I'm not one."

"I can't write about an historic incident until I research it fully and completely."

How much research do you think Leonardo da Vinci did before he painted *The Last Supper*? Of course he knew the story, from the Bible. But there are no physical descriptions of that scene or those individuals anywhere in any credible book.

Da Vinci knew *The Last Supper*. He knew it as well as if not better than any biblical source written decades after the fact. He knew it in his heart. Not in his head, which would have cautioned him against attempting anything so out of his experience, but in his heart. He had lived the emotions he represented and those emotions are the only truth in that masterful painting.

So you've never experienced the discrimination a black woman or gay man might have felt? Have you ever been attacked for who you are? Have you ever been denied what you believed was rightfully yours? Have you ever felt your personhood and humanity under attack?

No? Think back to your childhood. Think back to the emotions of childhood, to the bullies in the schoolyard, to the adults who criticized you. Do more than think back. Relive and re-experience those emotions. You have lived some of those same emotions you feel you dare not describe in someone else.

Accept the dare. Step up to the challenge. You owe it to yourself to at least try. For if any character — however far removed from your life and lifestyle — comes to you and demands that his or her story be told through you, then you can only trust that all you need lies within you.

Of course, research may be required. Remember, though, that unless you are writing a dry recitation of history, it's the emotions that will touch your readers, that will affect them, that will move them to deeper places within themselves. And we all — whether we're black, white, green or purple — draw from the same pool of emotions.

If you can give yourself permission to tap into that pool within you, you will always write what you know. For all you need to know lies within you. Now. At this moment.

Write what you know — what you know in your deepest heart. Write your fire. Write your truth.

The only knowledge that's unique to you is the knowledge of your heart, the wisdom of your soul, the force of your passion. Write from those places that no one else can and you will touch readers in ways that no one else can.

Go ahead and write what you know...if you dare.

Here's a suggestion...

Write on the Muse Stream from any or all of these key phrases:

- I know fear...

- I know humiliation...

- I know betrayal...

- I know what it feels like to be different...

- I know what it feels like to be attacked...

- I know what it feels like to be judged...

Let it be a story from your childhood, from your adolescence or from your present. Or let it be a creation of your inner vision. Whichever it is, write what you know. Write from your heart, write what your Muse tells you. Surrender to that knowingness and let the true emotions, true passion and true truth of your soul be unleashed onto the page.

Alternatively, turn the page and let the meditation *Write the Feeling* help guide you through the experience.

Write the Feeling

Guided Meditation #5

For optimal results, record this guided meditation and play it back for your own use, or have a friend read it to you. A version recorded by the author is also available on The Voice of the Muse Companion CD *(see page 35).*

Relax...close your eyes...and breathe. Let your shoulders drop. Let them drop some more. Then some more.

Feel your jaw loosen and relax. Yawn, opening your mouth as wide as you can, holding it open as long as you can. Move your head around and clear the kinks from your neck.

Again, let your shoulders drop.

Through it all, continue to breathe. Breathe in calm and quiet. Breathe out fears, fatigue, stress. Breathe in to a quiet place...a quiet time. A quiet place where you feel free to remember, free to see.

Breathe. In and out. In and out. In and out.

See yourself, now, stepping from this place, this room in which you now rest, and onto an elevator. The elevator door opens and you enter.

You're alone on this elevator. There are only two floor buttons. The top button is for the floor you're on. It's marked "N" for now, for this present moment, for the adult you are. Below it is a button marked "P." "P" for the past, for a moment in your past, for the adolescent you were, the child you were.

Reach out now and press "P," for a moment in your past.

The door closes and the elevator begins to move. You feel it descending, slowly dropping...going down, going back...going down, going back — to other times, other places.

As the elevator goes down and back, let your mind go back with it. Back to a time when you were very young. Maybe 4 years old, or 5 or 6. As far back as you can remember.

Perhaps it's a moment you hold in your conscious memory. Or a moment that is new to you. A moment that happened to you in this lifetime, or a moment from some distant past, a moment that stands as a powerful metaphor.

Regardless, let yourself be drawn there. Don't resist or second-guess. Say "yes" to whatever comes...to whatever age or time comes to you. Whatever it is.

You're back in a time when something happened.

Something significant.

Something important.

Something that carries an emotional charge. A time that reaches out to you right now and draws you back to it. Perhaps it was a time of great fear...or great joy. Of profound humiliation...or intense loving. A time of betrayal...or loyalty. Of tragedy or delight.

Whatever it was, whenever it was, that moment has a charge to it. A powerful charge. Something happened. Something happened that draws you back to it.

Back into it.

Now the elevator door opens and you step out. You step out into that moment, into that setting, into that scene. Not as the individual and age you are today, but as whoever you were in that moment, that moment of great charge, that moment in the past that calls to you.

So you step out of the elevator, not looking back in memory...not analyzing it from your present-day perspective. You step out *into* that moment...as whoever you were in that moment. Into the experience. You're in it now. As it's happening.

Perhaps you see it vividly, in color, with lots of detail. Perhaps you don't see it clearly, but you feel or sense it deeply. However it comes is the right way for you.

So you step out of the elevator and into the past.

Whatever the experience, know that you are safe. Know that at any time, should you feel unsafe, in danger or unable to cope, you can get back onto the elevator, press "N" for now and return to the present time.

Right now, though, you're still in the past, back as whoever you were when something happened. Back to wherever that something happened.

How old are you? Where are you? Who is with you? What is happening?

And now, now what is happening?

See it. Feel it. Sense it. Be in it completely. Experience it fully.

Are you in the city or the country? Are you inside or outside? Note the colors. The smells. The textures. The sounds. The quality of the light.

What's the weather like?

Absorb your surroundings. Take in the experience. The whole experience.

What are you doing? Who is with you? What do they look like? How old are they? What are they doing?

If something isn't clear, let it go. Maybe it's not important. Maybe it will come later.

Just take whatever comes and move on to see whatever you see. To feel whatever you feel. To sense whatever you sense. To experience whatever you experience.

Now, what are you doing?

And now what is happening?

Now, what are you feeling?

And now?

This is a way to immerse yourself into the emotions of a situation, to feel it fully, experience it completely, so that you can translate that emotion, that feeling, into whatever you're writing, whenever you're writing it.

So see it. Feel it. Experience it.

Don't judge. Don't analyze. Just be with it. Be in it. Know it, again.

Allow yourself forty-five seconds to complete this experience, which is all the clock time you will need.

Now, take a few breaths to complete the experience. To feel all there is to feel. To see all there is to see. To know all there is to know. To thank or heal or say goodbye.

When you feel complete, turn around, away from the scene you have just experienced. You're facing the elevator door again. It's open and you step in, pressing "N" for now, for the present moment. The door closes and the elevator begins to rise

Feel it rise as you slowly return to the age you are now, to this day, this time, this moment, this space.

Take all the time you need to return to the present. The door will open as you open your eyes. It will open only when you're ready.

When you feel ready, write about what you felt, saw, experienced. Let it be a vignette, a story, a poem. Let it be a memory. Let it be what it is, whatever it is. Let the form emerge by itself.

Don't force it. Never force it.

If you can, write it as the person you were when you experienced the event. Use the present tense if that helps you retain the immediacy, force and emotion of the event.

Write it in whatever way feels right for you. Write the feelings of the moment, the experiences of the moment. Write *in* the moment.

Remember not to edit or censor. Just allow whatever comes out to come out, in whatever way it needs to.

As always, keep your pen moving on the page. If you're stuck, remember to use repetition, free-association, nonsense words or doodling. Remember to breathe.

And keep writing. Keep writing until you feel complete...taking all the time you need.

Everything You Write Has Value

You believe that what you've written today is at best self-indulgent or repetitious, at worst irrelevant. So be it. It's okay to think that. As long as you don't allow your thoughts to stop you from continuing.

Every word that emerges in every writing session has its own contribution to make to your book or project...or life — be it a direct or indirect one. Trust that and stay open to the flow.

I'm not asking you to trust that this word is perfect and that so is this one. I'm asking you to trust that this word forms part of a larger pattern that you will not be able to see until you step back from it — later today, tomorrow, next week, next month or next year. Until you do, you are in no position to discern or determine anything, certainly not to judge anything.

You open a jigsaw puzzle box and toss its contents onto the floor. All you have is a collection of oddly shaped pieces that seem to go nowhere, connect with nothing — like your thoughts, like your words as you sit down to write, like the first draft of your manuscript. Yet slowly, as you fit two pieces together, then ten, then thirty, a pattern emerges.

In your writing, too, a pattern will emerge.

Nothing of what you write is irrelevant. Anything that finds its way from heart to hand to page is relevant. Remember that.

Trust — in the moment, in the word of the moment, in the fact that in the moment you cannot yet see or imagine how the words will string together to form a cogent and coherent whole. But this moment leads to the next and to the next. Then, out of all those moments, an hour forms, then a day, then a week, then a month, then a year, then a lifetime. And you discover, in looking back, that the moments that were the building blocks of that larger whole were integral to it, perhaps in ways you could not have known at the time. And that without them, there would have been no whole.

So trust. Trust that there is sense and wholeness — hidden from you, perhaps, in this moment but ready to reveal itself at any time...and likely to reveal itself sooner than later when you listen to your heart.

Do you still believe that you have nothing new to say? Nothing of value? Everything you write is original, if it comes from your place of authenticity.

It doesn't matter if you look at the moon with a group of 5,000 writers also looking at the moon. What the moon means to you in that instant will be unique and original if you allow yourself to hear, trust and record the uniqueness and originality that flow from your heart at that precise moment. If you do, your words will move, delight or offend the readers it needs to.

Other moon-words serve other readers. Others' heart-stories — about growing up or love or kids or war or betrayal or hatred or redemption — will touch whomever they need to touch. As will yours.

Whatever you write from your place of authenticity is unique, regardless of what you have read or been told. For your heart, though connected to every other, is not every other. If it were, we would need only one book, one piece of music, one painting, one style of architecture and one style of fashion.

Your heart is different. It is touched by different things. It is moved by different expressions of the human emotions that move us all.

Your expression will touch others in ways you cannot imagine.

Once again, this is all predicated on your level of trust. Do you trust your truth enough to heed and record it? Do you trust yourself enough to go to the place of connection where you can hear it? These are your starting points. This is your life. Write it. Now.

Here's a suggestion:

Team up with a writing partner and write on the Muse Stream from the same key word or phrase. Agree on one from *Fifty Keys to Unlock Your Writing* (page 40) or take turns choosing one.

When you're done, share your writing (without judgment or self-criticism) and see how different your truth is from your partner's.

Before sharing, read *Creative Support* (Chapter 14). Have your partner read it too. Expand the experience to a larger group by forming a Voice of the Muse Writers Circle (see *Creative Connection*, page 221).

The Song of Your Heart

You're afraid? Then you do not believe that your heart is a safe place. You do not believe that any place is a safe place.

Your heart is such a place. Your heart is where your truth resides. Your heart is the smartest brain, strongest muscle, most developed tool in your body. Your heart is your connection to your Muse, to your divinity.

Your brain is not that muscle, though it possesses the essential tools to translate that connection onto the page. Your brain is not that connecting place. Your heart is.

Your heart is connected to every other heart in the cosmos. Every one. Your heart is connected to every thought, every motion, every emotion, every nuance, every breath in all of Creation. Imagine that.

Stop a minute and place your hand on your heart. Feel the beat. Feel the rhythm. Feel the drumbeat that calls out to every other drumbeat. Know that each beat carries a message. Each beat carries a tune. Each beat sings the unique song of your soul to every other soul.

No, you don't have to put that song into words on a page. But if you didn't long to, if part of you didn't cry out to connect in writing, then you wouldn't be sitting here, turning the pages of this book in wonder, fear, excitement or awe.

Not awe at these words of my heart. Awe at the power of yours.

For my heart speaks no more powerfully than does yours. No heart speaks more powerfully, eloquently or truthfully than any other.

What distinguishes one human from another is not the song in his or her heart, it's the trust in that song and in that heart. It's trusting that by freeing your heart song onto the page, you will have performed a godlike act of creation.

Here's a suggestion:

Again, place your hand on your heart and feel its rhythm. Close your eyes and focus all your attention on the beat. Breathe into it and think of it as an ancient tribal drum sending a message to the next village.

You are the next village. What is the message for you today? What does the drumbeat of your heart say?

Listen.

Listen for the song of your heart. Listen for its rhythm and its words. Listen and write what you hear. Write on the Muse Stream.

Alternatively, use this key phrase to launch your writing: "I hear the drumbeat of my heart..."

6.

The Myth of Writer's Block

And the day came when the risk
to remain tight in a bud was more painful than
the risk it took to blossom.

ANAÏS NIN

It is not because things are difficult
that we do not dare; it is because we do not dare
that things are difficult.

SENECA

There Is No Writer's Block / I

There is no writer's block. There is only fear. When we stare at the blank page, the only marks on it the beads of saltwater sweat that drip from our stressed, frustrated brows, we are not experiencing a lack of talent. We are experiencing a fear so primal it has probably been with us at least since childhood.

It has probably been with us since that first time someone judged us harshly or devalued us in some way. It happens all the time and it happens, more often than not, from a misapplication of love than from love's absence.

Whatever the past created, the present can transform. Writing can transform your pain into joy, your fear into love...into aloha.

Why do you feel blocked? Because you fear to travel where your pen would guide you. Because you're afraid to surrender to the unknown gifts that await you. Because you're afraid to let go of all the controls that bind you to a place that feels safe but isn't.

Meet Annie. Annie was in her late fifties when she attended her first class of mine. Short, with close-cropped graying hair, she had a pixie's frame but lacked a pixie's spark.

"I want to write a memoir," she announced when we introduced ourselves, each word measured, controlled. "But I have writer's block. I have had it for a decade."

She struggled with the early exercises, struggled against the controls she had placed on her self-expression. She wanted to avoid going where her pen was taking her, wanted to force her pen in other directions.

Yet as she surrendered to her pen and, perforce, to that pixie part of herself that was now, at last, finding expression, she had everyone in the room laughing so hard at the absurdities of her Earth Mother alter ego, we couldn't stop crying.

Annie, and that's not her real name, didn't have writer's block. She was afraid to embrace the part of herself that was light, funny, bizarre and uncontrollable. Once she did, her self-described block dissolved in a rush of daily writing — just for the pleasure of seeing where it would take her, just for the joy of surrender.

Here's a suggestion:

Write on the Muse Stream, beginning with this phrase: "I follow my pen wherever it carries me. Today, it carries me to…"

After you've written:

Where did you end up? Was it difficult to let your pen be in charge? What did you discover on the journey? Write about that.

New Rhythms, New Routines

Because so much of my writing history at the time I created *The MoonQuest* was linked to desks, deadlines and other people's projects, the only way I could banish old associations that felt anything but free-flowing was to break all the patterns of my previous writing life.

First I abandoned the computer, composing *The MoonQuest*'s early drafts with pen and paper. Next, I abandoned my desk, bound as it was to the soul-numbing words that had so recently comprised my livelihood.

Mornings, with a pad balanced on my knee, just before or after breakfast, I allowed *The MoonQuest*'s scenes to pour from my pen onto the blank page. Evenings, I input the day's jottings into the computer.

Some days I needed a more dramatic break from the old to connect with my nascent story. On those days I often drove over North Mountain to Baxter Harbour on the Bay of Fundy. There, as the Atlantic surf crashed on the rocky Nova Scotia shore, I sat in the car or on a boulder and let the ocean tell me what to write next. A one-day change of habit and venue was all it took to put me back on track.

Here's a suggestion:

When you feel blocked, break the pattern of your normal routine. If you normally write on the computer, switch to pen and paper. Write in the morning instead of the afternoon or evening, or vice versa. If you tend to write at your desk, move away from the perceived pressures of your "work" environment. Go for a walk to clear your mind. Take pad and pen and curl up in a comfortable chair. Sit out in nature. Move to a favorite café. Drive to some place quiet...different...inspirational. And feel the creative power of your new rhythm.

What Is It You Fear? / *I*

What is it you fear? Is it the power of your voice? The power of your words? The power of your truth?

These are worthy of awe not fear. Fear suggests danger. Yet your voice, words and truth bring you nothing but safety.

You seek safety outside yourself. You seek safety by keeping your light buried deep within — so deep that even you don't always know it's there.

That light is your safety. That light is your protection.

Lies cannot save you. Only truth can save you: the truth that lies within your heart, the truth that is your heart...waiting, longing, yearning to find expression.

For a writer, that expression takes shape through letters, words and sentences on a page. Commit the truth of your heart to the page and you commit to yourself as the writer you are. Commit that truth to the page and you free it from the prison of your fear.

What is it you fear? Is it the unknown? Is it the word that lies within you, buried so deeply you dare not disturb it from its slumber? It sleeps not. It waits, patiently, for the moment of your courage. It waits for the key that lies in your hand, the key to your heart, your truth and your courage.

Take that key. Feel its weight. Study its curves and notches. See the brilliance of its metal. Know it this one last time. Know what it has saved you from in the past and what it holds you back from today. Thank it for the former but don't curse it for the latter. It is but a piece of metal and carries no blame.

You are your own jailer. No one but you. Don't curse yourself or your fear. Forgive yourself and your fear.

Forgive yourself and allow what has been to have been. Allow it and know it is of the past. Locks and keys had their place in that past. They have no place in your present. They cannot follow you into your future.

Fit the key into that lock that shuts your heart, that shuts you and the world from your heart. Fit the key into that lock and turn it.

Do you feel resistance? Don't force it. Don't force anything. Allow it to turn. Will it to turn. Invite it to turn. See it turn. Hear the latch click as the lock opens, the door swings wide and light pours forth. The light of your heart, your heart's truth, floods through you and out into the world. And the light of the world's beauty courses through you.

You are joined, connected, united, and the words can flow now — safely, freely, openly, lovingly and compassionately — first onto the page, the page that exists for your eyes only, and later, when you're ready, when the filters of your discernment guide you, out into the world.

For now, though, the very act of setting words to paper frees them into the world, even if no one sees them but you. For they have moved from one realm to another, from the unconscious world to the conscious, from the inner world to the outer and, in so doing, touch others through that realization.

How? Your words change you. Your words released onto the page free you in ways you cannot fully see. What you cannot see still exists. What you cannot yet see in yourself, others will see.

They will not know that words have freed you. They will not know why you shine more brilliantly today than yesterday. But your light will touch them, long before they hear or read the words you have written. And they, too, will be changed.

Here's a suggestion:

Write on the Muse Stream, using any or all of these phrases to launch your writing journey:

- I am the key. I am the key to...

- Each of my words is a light that...

- I free my words onto the page and into the world. In doing that I free myself to...

After you've written:

How do you feel now that you've written? Are you aware of any changes? Physical? Emotional? If you do, write about them. If you don't, don't judge — either yourself or your words. Simply congratulate yourself for having written, and do something special for yourself in celebration of that achievement.

You're Stuck

You're stuck. Your fingers hover in paralysis over your keyboard. Your fist grips your pen so tightly that nothing can move forward.

You're stuck. Neither fingers nor fist are the true culprits. They are mindless accessories to a single-minded mind that has set up flares, roadblocks, chain-link fences and walls beyond which no pen or pixel may tread.

Danger appears to lie beyond that barrier, that block which, moments ago, did not exist. Yet it exists now.

Where did it come from? Where is the perceived danger? Is it visible from your point of stuckness, or does it lie just beyond the bend in the road now closed before you?

I have known this sense of danger. I live with it now as I pen these words. It, too, would keep me from moving forward — on this page, in my life, on my journey.

What is it you fear? Ask the question, but don't wait for an answer. Keep writing. Allow your pen the freedom to keep dancing across the paper. Allow your fingers the freedom to keep dancing across the keyboard. Allow the words, your heart words, to keep dancing across your page or screen. Allow.

You're stuck. My words sound good, but you're still stuck.

Try this: Keep your pen and fingers dancing, regardless of what flows from them. If you're afraid, write your fears. Exposing them to the light of day and the air of your breath will dilute and dissipate them, allowing you to write through and past them.

Thank that part of you that is in fear. Thank it, for it is not malignant and is no demon. Thank it for protecting you in the past when you needed protection.

Once, it protected us from being scorched and consumed in the fire of a truth we were not yet ready to live, let alone write...to write, let alone live.

Now, though, we are ready, not to move through life without protection, but with more discerning filters, ready to open the gate wider to allow life's experiences more access to our hearts and our hearts more access to the page.

Ask that fearful part of you to be less fearful and more discerning. Tell it you're ready. Tell yourself you're ready. For you are. Ready. Now. To tell your story. To speak your truth, to write your story...whatever it is.

Reach for your pen. Place your fingers on the keyboard. Start writing. Then keep writing — on the Muse Stream. Write into the stuckness... through the stuckness...past the stuckness.

Just write.

Now.

Talk to Your Block

Dialogue is a potent tool for connecting with those parts of you that are holding back your writing...or your life.

My most memorable experience of the power of dialogue occurred some years back after a profoundly disturbing dream. In the dream I'm on foot, trying to leave an underground parking garage. But the uniformed attendant won't let me pass.

I argue. He argues back.

I shout. He shouts back.

Everything I say or do is met with unyielding resistance.

I'm stuck.

A few days later in meditation, I call this surly guard back into my consciousness. When once again he blocks my exit, I ask, calmly and compassionately, "Why won't you let me out?"

As we dialogue back and forth, he tells me that his job is to protect me. "If I let you leave," he says, "I'll be out of work."

I reassure him that I still need his protection, but in new ways. He agrees to learn to act more as a filter than a block.

When we're done, we shake hands and embrace. I walk past him and out into the sunlight, knowing I can move forward now...safely.

Here's a suggestion:

Remember the dialogue with your critic (*Taming Your Critic*, page 71)? This is a similar exercise. But instead of interacting with your critic, you'll be engaging with a part of you that is blocked, perhaps the one shut down by your critic.

It's as simple as getting into a meditative space and entering into a written conversation with a blocked part of yourself. As I did with my garage attendant, ask your questions without emotional charge and allow the answers to flow to you on the Muse Stream.

Start by asking that part of you to identify itself and explain why it is holding you back from writing. Thank it for protecting you in the past and reassure it that it's still necessary, but in new ways.

Ask it to now be more of a filter and less of a block. Ask for its help, but remember to keep the powerful, fearless part of you in charge.

Use these and/or your own questions and allow the writing to come naturally. Don't force the answers. Don't judge or censor. Remember to breathe. Remember to turn to *If You Get Stuck* (page 32) should you need help.

- Who are you?

- Why don't you want me to write?

- Why don't you want me to write on [*name of project*]?

- Do you have a name?

- What are you afraid of?

- What can I do to reassure you?

- What would make you feel safer?

- How can I retrain you? How can you become less blocking and more discerning? How can you become less of a wall and more of a filter?

If you don't get all the answers you seek in one session, rejoin the conversation again another day, and another, if necessary.

Your Words Are Your Teachers / I

Your words are your teachers. Listen to your words, those that issue from your lips as much as those that leap onto the page. Listen to your words and to all they reveal about your creative enterprise, to all they reveal about your life's enterprise.

Watch yourself today. Notice the many times you judge yourself...or others.

Start with yourself. For you will no longer judge others once you stop judging yourself. Yes, this book is about writing. But judgment is a key to the very block that holds back your words.

Listen to your words, but don't censor yourself. Don't take the whip to yourself for every word you free out into the world. Don't allow with your heart and then beat up with your head. Listen to yourself and learn.

Here are some words and phrases to listen and learn from:

- *pointless*, as in "What I'm writing is pointless."

- *control*, as in "I need to be in control of this story" or "I need to control this process."

- *order, sequence*, as in "I need to write this in order" or "I can't write sections out of sequence."

- *trying*, as in "I'm trying to make time to write" or "I'm trying to write every day."

- *impossible*, any use, unless preceded by the word "not."

- *hard, difficult, challenging*, as in "It's hard because..." or "It's difficult to..." or "It's challenging to..."

- *not enough*, as in "not good enough" or "not creative enough" or "not enough time."

- *block* or *blocked*, as in "I have writer's block" or "I'm blocked."

- *not as good as*, as in "What I wrote is not as good as what Joe (or Shakespeare or anyone) wrote" or "What I wrote today is not as good as what I wrote yesterday."

- *can't*, as in "I can't write" or "I can't write well" or "I can't write now" or "I can't write/say that."

- *supposed to*, in any context.

- *should*, in any context.

- *just* or *only*, as in "This is just a journal entry" or "This is just a first draft" or "I've only written 500 words. Or fifty. Or five…"

Now, focus on some of these instead. *Surrender.* Now there's a word. *Release.* That's a powerful one. *Let go…*great phrase. How about *fly free*? Or *leap of faith*? How about *trust*? Or *allow*? Or *I can*? Or *I will*? Or *I am*? How about *possible, doable, now*?

How about focusing on what you have accomplished not on what is lacking from your work? How about reminding yourself that you are a writer…and a powerful one? How about remembering that everything is not only possible, but as easy as you will allow it to be?

As you do that, you will birth more creative excellence than you could ever produce by worrying, judging, diminishing and deriding whatever random writings, musings and jottings first issue from your pen.

Listen to your words. Hear what they tell you about what you think and believe. Then begin to transform those thoughts and beliefs by choosing new words. Train yourself to be more conscious and you'll open to a fuller experience and expression of the writer you are.

Here's a suggestion:

As you move through the rest of your day, be more conscious of your words and thoughts. Correct yourself gently, with love, when what you speak or think is critical, diminishing, judgmental or unsupportive — of yourself or others — or when your words or thoughts deny your infinite potential, innate creativity or inner vision.

Let your words be your teachers, and learn from them.

What Is It You Fear? / *II*

What is it you fear? What words, thoughts and images lie deep within you that you have imprisoned there? Which words, thoughts and images do you fear could destroy you if you allowed them the freedom to float up and fly out of you? What is so dangerous?

Perhaps, once upon a time in this life or another, you were locked away for your words. Perhaps you were harmed or killed. Part of you was certainly wounded enough to prevent you from speaking out again.

The past is passed. It no longer exists. It no longer has the potential or power to harm you...unless you choose to let it.

Too often, we live our present from a vantage point of the past. Too often, we run all our present experiences and future possibilities through a filter of the past rather than standing in this moment.

Ask yourself what it is you fear from the words that lie trapped within. Ask the question and write the answer and, in so doing, free yourself from the grip of those fears. And in so doing, you will free your words, your truth and yourself to soar, to fly, to be.

Be. Be the writer you are by writing all that lies within you. Be the human being you are, the spiritual and creative being you are, by opening to all possibilities, all words and all worlds.

Set your words free. Lower the drawbridge and open the castle gate. Do that and watch the words flow out of your once-fortified heart, onto the page and out into the world. That is where they belong. That is where you belong: out, open and free.

What is it you fear? Ask the question and write the answer.

Write the answer and release it. Release it and feel the nervous excitement that freedom brings.

Feel the pounding heart, the butterfly stomach. Your heart pounds the freedom of the surf as it ebbs and flows on its infinite series of meetings with the shore. Your stomach flits the powerful but uncertain wings of the butterfly just emerged from its cocoon.

Let the waves roar your truth. Fly on those wings. They will seem unsure at first. But with each foray, each exploration, each journey of pen across the page, they will strengthen and gain in confidence. And the fears, now past, will free you into the present and prepare you for the future. Present words. Future words. God's words spoken and expressed through you.

You don't believe in God? That doesn't matter. If a universal spirit or energy moves through all beings, it must move through all words. For words are beings, too — beings and expressions of being, all at the same time.

Don't worry about where this or anything you might write is going. Let it go, and it will carry you to your destination.

Your words are your teachers. Your words are your guides. Let them teach you as they guide you from one sentence to the next, from one adventure to the next, from one journey to the next.

Allow them this role. Release your controlling personality mind from its natural desire to take on this role. Release it to the words, the words that will take form and shape on your page.

Allow them that role and you will travel to worlds beyond your conscious imagining, worlds of richness and depth that will surprise you, may scare you, will touch you — so deeply you may not, at first, be aware of having been touched. Touched and changed: for that's what heart words do. Heart words touch and transform you and, having emerged from a place of depth, truth and trust, they will touch and transform others.

The Butterfly

Guided Meditation #6

For optimal results, record this guided meditation and play it back for your own use, or have a friend read it to you. A version recorded by the author is also available on The Voice of the Muse Companion CD *(see page 35).*

Close your eyes. Breathe in deeply, fully. Allow your shoulders to drop, and drop some more. And some more. Allow yourself to relax. Fully.

From that place of calm, let your breath transport you into the realm of imagination, the realm of creativity, the realm of vision.

See yourself now in another form, another body. A caterpillar's body.

You're a caterpillar, enfolded in a cocoon. Like a blanket-bundled infant or your blanket-bundled sleep-in self, you're enveloped in the divine caress of in-between time.

In this moment, you're safe. Safe in the all-embracing darkness. Secure in the womb of creation, transformation, rebirth.

Creation. Transformation. Rebirth.

Feel that transformation within you. Feel your shape begin to shift. Feel your body lighten and wings begin to form.

Feel the nascent emergence of color, translucence, delicacy.

Now, feel the pressure of your wings as, pressed between your body and the walls of the cocoon, they begin to push and spread, push and spread. Push and spread.

Such delicate wings, yet so strong. So strong.

Such a delicate body, yet so strong. So strong.

So awake. So determined. So ready.

What was once a sanctuary is now stifling. What once held you in safety now presses against you, holds you down. Holds you back.

Thank the cocoon and the caterpillar you were for letting you sleep, for keeping you safe, for holding you secure. Thank them and release them from the need to do so any longer.

Now it's time to awaken.

Now it's time to fly.

Now it's time to be a creature of earth and sky. Of sky and earth. Now it's time to travel great distances, to soar to great heights, to stretch the limits of the possible. To enter into the realm of the improbable, the realm of the impossible.

Feel the walls of your cocoon begin to give way. Feel your wings begin to spread as they push and push and push some more.

It's hard work, at times, to push free of the barriers we have created for ourselves. But we always have the strength. We always have the will. We always have the power.

All we need to do is acknowledge our strength, surrender to our highest imperative and allow our power to have its way with us.

It's time to surrender. To the butterfly you are. To the creator you are. To the free-flowing, free-flying being you are. So do it.

Push one last time with those wings that seem so delicate but carry the strength and will of the universe. Push one last time and feel the walls of your cocoon break apart. Now, spread your wings to the fullness of their span and fly free.

Fly free.

Fly free.

Now.

You may feel tentative, uncertain. Shaky. That's normal. These are new wings, new experiences, new expressions. Allow the uncertainty, knowing that with each flight you *will* become more certain, more practiced, more adept.

Fly for as long as you like. Explore your new world from this new perspective. Take your time. And when you're ready to light down again — on a flower petal, on a leaf or on a blank sheet of paper that has fluttered to earth — open your eyes and write about your experiences, your feelings, your journey.

Write about them *as* the caterpillar-turned-butterfly, describing your transformation, your liberation, your flight.

And write about them as the writer you are, now free of one more barrier to your freest, fullest expression.

Soul Authorship

You ask why you fear the blank page even as you know that the act of writing will make you feel better. It's simple: The fear of the void far outweighs any perceived benefit that might arise from allowing it to be filled.

There's the key: the *allowing*.

It's allowing the void to be filled that is the challenge. Writing is an act of allowing, of allowing your creative spirit to speak through you, of allowing your Muse its voice.

Allowing doesn't mean that you don't participate in the act, that you switch yourself off and allow a Muse-like entity to speak through you. Creation is not a hands-off act. You *are* involved.

You cannot help but be involved, at every stage of the enterprise. Your conscious mind has various levels and degrees of involvement, depending on the stage. Yet your unconscious mind, which expresses the words and truths of your heart, is always involved. It works with your spirit, God, Muse or creative source to bring these words into the physical realm.

You must surrender. Yes. But not abstain. Nor can you abstain from responsibility for the words you allow to form on the page. It's a fine line. Are you involved or not involved? Are you channeling or creating? Whose book is it anyway?

The answer is not simple. Everything is a cocreative act. Energies are working with you all the time. Even the most conscious act of creation is not yours alone. Nor is the most unconscious act totally separate from you. There is a quantum oneness that's always at work.

Everything and everyone is connected to everyone else and everything else. When that is so, there is no sole authorship, only soul authorship.

Your words are as much your words as not your words, as much not your words as your words. It's a concept that is neither simple nor complex. It is what it is, in all the simplicity and complexity of the universe.

Resistance Is Futile

Resistance is futile. You seek to hide. There is no hiding. You seek to escape. There is no escape.

There is only your truth. There is only your heart. And although you can try to hide from them, you can't escape, for they will follow you to the ends of the earth and will ultimately have their way with you.

So why not surrender, now? The pain is in the resistance. The so-called writer's block is in the resistance.

Writer's block is nothing more nor less than your resistance to those words that would have their way with you if you would but surrender to them. Instead, you say, "No, not these words. I want others."

Well, there are no other words. There are only heart words.

If you would but open your heart and allow what longs to flow from you easy egress, there would be no block. If you would but make your fear subservient to your courage, there would be no block. For fear and courage can coexist, but not as equals. One must take precedence. Fear leads to inaction. Courage to action. Fear and courage evenly matched lead to paralysis, which is the same as inaction.

So, still your judge. Just for this moment. Now for this one. Now for this one. And now for this one. And maybe, now, for this one, too.

Still that part of yourself that would judge you, your words or both to be unworthy, silly, without merit, laughable. Still that part of yourself that fears being opened to ridicule...or worse.

Nothing will happen to you for putting words on a page. No one can harm you, no matter how outrageous your words or thoughts, for what flows from you onto the page.

Ah, but I hear, "I don't want to see myself saying, thinking, writing... believing those words that want to get onto the page." That's a different matter, one you must face.

Do you want to write truth, the truth from which both powerful fiction and nonfiction arise? If you want to write truth, if you want to write words that will touch the deepest emotions and connections and truths of your reader, then you must write what your heart calls on you to write. You must answer the call of your Muse.

You must first still yourself enough to listen. You must then trust enough to listen — trust yourself and trust your heart. Finally, you must gather all the courage you possess, which is many, many times more than you in this moment believe you possess, and record what you hear. You must let the words fall from heart to hand to page. You must let them flow. For within them lies the truth, your truth. It is that truth that will change the world, beginning with your world.

Perhaps that is where the fear comes from, a fear you may not understand or know you possess. Perhaps. If it be so, then know that when you accept the call to write, you accept the call to change your life.

The mere act of sitting in silence in front of a blank page or screen is a life-changing and life-affirming experience. The mere presence of that vacuum, which you have created and are trusting your Muse to fill, is a life-changing experience.

Let me repeat that: *The mere act of sitting down to write is a life-changing experience.*

So why would it come as a surprise to discover that the words themselves will change you?

Why do we write? To discover what we believe, what we know, who we are. Just as we live, day to day, moment to moment, to discover those things. If it is change you fear, then you will face writer's block. Stopping the flow of change-words stops the flow of all words.

What is it you fear? That you will discover what you think or believe? That setting those thoughts or beliefs to paper is an unbreakable commitment to them?

Nothing you think or believe in this moment is fixed for all time. It is true in this moment alone. It may still be true in the next, or it may not be.

Do not be afraid of change — in your writing or in yourself. Let each moment be a lifetime, complete in itself, just as each word is. Live it fully, and then move on to the next, knowing that, in the next moment, your story, your book, your life could change beyond recognition.

Let that lifetime unfold when it will. For now, be in this moment, with its unfolding words, thoughts and beliefs. For now, let your resistance dissolve on the Muse Stream of creativity.

Here's a suggestion:

Write on the Muse Stream from any or all of these phrases —

- In this moment, I fear...

- In this moment, I know...

- In this moment, I am free to...

After you've written:

Did you discover anything new? Anything surprising? Allow yourself your moment of discovery, of *re*discovery, freeing each revelation to be true in the moment you receive it, freeing yourself to continue changing beyond it in the moments yet to come.

The Breath of Creativity

Are you breathing? In your terror or excitement have you forgotten to breathe? Writing at its truest is an act of meditation. And meditation, whatever the form, relies upon breath.

Are you stuck? Does word not follow word with ease? Does fear poke its pointy head between one word and the next?

Breathe.

Write "I am breathing" and breathe that sentence onto the page as you write it. Inhale "I am breathing in" onto the page. Then exhale "I am breathing out." All of it onto the page, in alignment with your breath.

Breathe out the fear and breathe in the story. Breathe out the stuckness and breathe in a clear path to the next word, whatever it may be.

Writing — as all creativity, as all life — is an act of allowing. Allow your breath to come, allow your breath to go. Be conscious of each intake and outflow. Become conscious by writing the words of your breath onto the page: "I am breathing in...I am breathing out."

Keep breathing. Keep writing your breath, the breath of creativity. And in no time your breath will return to its normal unconscious practice, and so will the outpouring of words.

Breathe, for in your breath resides your life. In your breath, too, resides your story.

Breathe your words onto the page and breathe life into your words. Do that and the story will take care of itself.

Here's a suggestion:

When you find yourself worrying about which word to write next, remember that each breath you breathe comes naturally, without thought or forcing. Write as you breathe, knowing that word will follow word, just as breath follows breath, as soon as you get out of the way. Write as you breathe: freely, unconsciously, unselfconsciously, flowingly.

Write the Fear

Our fears lie in layers within us. Strip away one, resolve it, and in time another will reveal itself.

You have dissolved many layers to reach this point on your creative path. You have resolved much, and yet...

What is it you still fear? Discover it, too, by writing it. Acknowledge it. Then let it go.

It is both the writing and the releasing that allows the true writing to emerge. You may write pages and pages and pages of fear before you reach the place of no-fear, the place of flow, the place of freedom, the place where your story or book resides.

What emerges when you get there may surprise you. Let it.

What is it you fear? Which word do you fear placing in front of you today? Which word do you fear placing in front of the world? Do you dare write the first letter? The second?

What do you still fear?

Write the question and let the answer write itself. Let the answers write themselves.

Of all those, which is the core fear? Or is the core another fear altogether?

Again, write the question and let the answer reveal itself to you on the Muse Stream.

What is your payoff for that fear, those fears? In other words, what do you gain from that fear? How does it act as an incentive? What dividends does it yield in your life?

Once again, write the question and let your pen spell out the answer.

Are you surprised by the answer? Sit with it for a few minutes before reading on.

Now, using the payoff as your key word or phrase, write on the Muse Stream for fifteen or twenty minutes — or longer, if that's what will free you to feel complete — and see what emerges.

When you're done, set your writing aside and breathe deeply as you inhale your freedom from another fear, as you exhale another block.

What was it you feared? Whatever it was no longer matters. You have released it onto the page, given it permission to breathe and watched its power over you melt away on that breath.

You are free now. Free to write. Free to breathe. Free to be.

There Is No Writer's Block / II

There is no writer's block. There is no need for a blank page to remain blank. There is no reason for words not to flow. They may not be the words you would choose from your personality mind. That is not a block. That is a choice.

Unfortunately, unless you allow the words that yearn to flow room and space, no others will likely flow. No others worth mentioning. No others that will have the power and impact and emotion and life and heart and truth of those you denied an exit visa from your heart to the page.

Let them go. Let them free. Let yourself free. When you do, there are no blocks.

So, set the tip of your pen to the page and begin. Just begin.

Don't stop. Don't think. Don't question. Don't second-guess. Don't criticize. Don't judge.

Allow. Allow the pen to move you. Allow the words to flow. For they will.

It may feel difficult at first. But that is the same difficulty you experience in childbirth. You push and you push and you push. You strain and you strain and you strain. Then, suddenly, creation is freed and flows through you.

The strain in writing is not your brain straining to find the right words. It's your brain straining to hold you back from the right words. Do not let it stop you. Do not let anything stop you. Write any time and at all times. Write when you would rather be sailing. Write when you would rather be cleaning your bathroom. Write when you would rather be cleaning your neighbor's bathroom. Write whenever you feel the slightest resistance to writing. That resistance is the power of your words trying to surge past the barriers you have erected against them.

Tear down the barricades, just this one time. Tear them down and let the flow surge from you. Try it once. Then try it again. And discover that the block you thought you had has not dissolved because it was never truly there. The words were always there because the words *are* always there.

All you have to do is allow them free reign over you. Give them the keys to the kingdom of your dreams, your visions, your truth. They will not let you down. They may surprise you. They may scare you. They will empower you.

The Right Idea

There are many good ideas out there in the ethers — ideas for books and screenplays, ideas for songs, articles and poems. Your friends will suggest them. Your partner will suggest them. Your logical mind will suggest them.

You'll see something or hear about something and you'll think, "Wouldn't that make a great story?" Maybe it would. Maybe it's yours to write. Maybe it's not.

There's a difference between a good idea and the right idea, between an idea that is anyone's for the taking and one that is uniquely yours, one that's right for you, right now.

Before you launch into a frenzy of research and writing, ask yourself: Is this what I'm called to write? Is this the call of *my* Muse, the story only I can tell? Or is this anyone's? Is this another good idea or is this the right idea for me?

Anyone can take a good idea and give it shape and substance. Some can do it better than you, some not as well.

Nobody can take the idea that sings to your soul and perform the kind of alchemy on it that you can. Only you can transform that idea into the one-of-a-kind gem it longs to be. That is why it, through your Muse, called to you...chose you.

Accept that you were chosen. Perform your magic. Let the right idea be the idea *you* write. Right now.

Here's a suggestion:

Move into a meditative space, a place of deep connection. Take a few deep breaths in and out. When you're relaxed, pick up your pen and write on the Muse Stream for twenty minutes using this as your opening sentence: "My Muse calls on me to write (about)..."

After you've written:

Were you surprised? Did you discover a new direction? A confirmation of an existing one? Did you uncover material for future writing sessions?

This is a helpful exercise any time you're not certain in which direction to take your writing.

Write What's Right...for Right Now

If you find yourself feeling blocked on a particular project, ask yourself whether what you're writing *is* the right idea for you right now.

Perhaps it's the right idea for someone else but not for you. Perhaps it will be the right idea for you at some future time. Or perhaps this project was right for you when you began it, but is no longer.

It's possible that you've outgrown it. It's also possible that you haven't fully grown into it.

I was a hundred pages into the first draft of *The MoonQuest* when I set it aside for what turned into a five-month hiatus. The day I returned to the book, I was afraid to reread those hundred pages. I was afraid the manuscript wasn't any good, and I was afraid I had outgrown it and would have to abandon it.

What I realized, once I began reading, was that *I* hadn't been ready to continue with *The MoonQuest* and that's why my Muse had cut me off when it did.

As it turned out, five months away from the book gave me the life experience I needed in order to be able to carry on. I began writing that same day and three months and 300 additional pages later, the first draft was done.

Sometimes, what seems a block is a matter of timing. Sometimes, it's just not the right idea. When we drop a project or leave it incomplete, we don't always know into which of those two categories it falls.

If your discernment tells you to let the project go, don't mourn the perceived waste of time and energy. Trust that you will either return to it when the time is right or that you've gained all you needed from the experience and can now move on to other writing.

A wrong idea isn't necessarily wrong for all time. But if it's wrong for right now, let it go and free yourself to write what's right. For you. Now.

7.

Creation

You may be disappointed if you fail, but
you are doomed if you don't try.

BEVERLY SILLS

Life is either a daring adventure, or nothing.

HELEN KELLER

The Creator You Are

You assume that creation is about bringing something into the world out of nothing or, at best, out of some raw material like clay or wood.

Creation is more than that. In creating, you are not fashioning something out of nothing.

When a new being is created from the loving union of a man and woman, has that being been created out of nothing? No. That being's spirit and soul were already present. But it took the loving union of two beings and the raw materials, if you will, of sperm and egg, to set in motion the miracle that would unite a soul with its newly forming body.

Such is the case, too, with your artistic heart-creations.

Just as the soul of a new human being is eternal and does not need to be created, for it already is, so the work you set out to realize does not need to be created, at least not in the "manufacturing" sense we commonly associate with the word "create."

The soul of your work already exists. In that soul is encoded its words and form. As you connect with that soul through whatever connecting practice you use, the words and form make themselves known to you.

You are not creating something from nothing. You are listening, connecting, breathing and focusing your heart-mind, not your brain-mind, on emptying yourself of all preconceptions save the true *pre*-conception: the energy before conception that awaits to be heard and emerge. That is your creation. You create an opening, so that what already exists can emerge into a form that also already exists.

A blank page means only that the page is blank. It does not mean that what you seek to create doesn't already exist. It does — in its completeness and in its perfection.

The more open you are to receive it, the fewer revisions you'll have to make. For when you are most open, the work comes to you most closely resembling and being exactly what it is in its perfection.

Some of the pieces in this book, for example, appear near to their original, untouched, first-draft form. For them, I was at my most connected with the spirit and energy of this book, with the voice of my Muse. Others underwent multiple rewrites. With them, some part of me held back, didn't trust, didn't allow, didn't fully surrender to the creation that was birthing through me. Some part of me wasn't ready.

That's okay — for me and for you.

I don't judge (mostly). I simply do my best, writing day by writing day, revision session by revision session, to hold the vision, hear the voice and trust the outcome.

Here's a suggestion:

Sit down to write. As you do so, commit to abandoning all preconceptions and surrendering to *pre*-conception.

Say aloud: "As the creator I am, I allow my words and work to emerge into their natural form and flow into *their* idea of perfection, not mine. I surrender to the story and let it flow."

Now...let it flow.

The Soul of Creation

Guided Meditation #7

For optimal results, record this guided meditation and play it back for your own use, or have a friend read it to you. A version recorded by the author is also available on The Voice of the Muse Companion CD *(see page 35).*

Relax. Close your eyes. Return to that meditative space where all is possible, where judgments are dissolved, where creativity is sovereign.

Feel again that place in your heart where the creator within you resides, that place through which your Muse speaks. That place of light and of life. That eternal place. That magical place.

That place where everything is possible. Where creation is possible. Where magic and mystery and spirit and flow are the natural and normal ways of being.

Breathe into that, into that space.

Breathe into the power of your voice, your heart, and the expression, through your voice, of your heart.

And voice becomes words. And words become scratches on a page that, with the miracle of creation, become a whole — sometimes in spite of you.

So, surrender to that place of miracle and magic. That place of creation.

Breathe into it deeply and become one with it. So that when you reach for your pen and touch it to the page, or set your fingers on the keyboard, the words flow effortlessly.

And remember how important it is, always, to go with whatever comes first into your mind, whatever flows from your heart to your hand.

Now, reach deep inside, past the censoring of your mind, past the fear of your personality self, and let a word or an image emerge that represents creation for you. The soul of creation.

Whatever that word or image is will be unique to you and to this moment. And it will be perfect.

Remember that what you write may be about this or about something else altogether. This word is a jumping-off point, a place of departure on a magical, miracle-filled journey that you will discover in the writing.

Surrender to the journey. Surrender to the word or image that launches it. Surrender to the story.

Allow yourself to be carried effortlessly and weightlessly, lovingly and supportively, in the embrace of your creativity, as you write this word on the page and allow it to take you into the realm of your divinity, the kingdom of your creation.

When you're ready, but only then, open your eyes, remaining in that place you now find yourself, and write down the word or image that came to you, that rose from deep within you.

Set it to paper, and allow it to be the launching pad for that rocket-propelled journey that takes you where you need to go, where deep in your heart you desire to go.

So, when you're ready, take off and go. Take off and write.

Remember to keep going, nonstop, until you sense completion — writing through and past all stuckness, allowing creation to birth through you and onto the page.

8.

Time to Write

Determine that the thing can and shall be done,
and then we shall find the way.

ABRAHAM LINCOLN

You must do the thing you think you cannot do.

ELEANOR ROOSEVELT

Now Is the Time to Write / II

Don't wait. Don't wait for the perfect moment or the perfect slice of time. Don't wait for your vacation or for your kids to grow up. Don't wait to fix up a special place in your home. Don't wait until your partner or spouse is out for the evening or away on business. Don't wait until you finish this paragraph.

Is your pen in hand? No? Pick it up. Turn to a fresh page in your notebook. Touch the nib to the writing surface. Write a word. Any word. Whatever flows from your pen. Don't think about it. Don't think about anything. Just write that one word. Then another. Then another.

The best time to write is now. The only time to write is now. All you need is twenty minutes. Even ten will do.

You don't know what to write? Pick a word or phrase from *Fifty Keys to Unlock Your Writing*, page 40. Any one.

Pick it. Write it. Now.

Then keep going.

Don't stop...not for any reason. Just keep placing one word after the next after the next after the next, until you're done.

How Much Did You Write?

How much did you write? How many words did you squeeze into those ten or twenty minutes? No, don't stop and count. Just be aware of the volume. Don't stop to reread or judge the quality; just notice the quantity. Now, can you ever honestly say you lack the time to write? How can you claim that when twenty minutes has wrought such output?

There is always time to write. There may not be as much as you would prefer. It may not appear in convenient places. But it's there. Waiting for you.

You can't find twenty minutes? Surely you can find ten in the interstices of life — while you're waiting in the doctor's office or during a lull at work. Carve it out of your lunch hour. Wake up ten minutes earlier. Go to sleep ten minutes later. The time is there. And the words, once you demonstrate your willingness to receive them, will cooperate, if you allow them to stream from your pen.

"Wait," I hear you say, "I don't write longhand. I can't read my handwriting. I can't write unless I'm on the keyboard."

Start training yourself to write on anything, with anything, anywhere. The words long to pour from you. Never doubt that. They yearn to spill from your heart onto the page. They don't need to wait for the right tool, the right time or the right place. You may think you need the right tool, the right time, the right place. The words don't. The moment you open to them, wherever you are, whatever you're using, they will come. Always.

What if ten minutes is more than you can manage on a given day? First, don't beat yourself up. Don't judge yourself as uncommitted or unworthy. Instead, take five minutes, or two minutes or thirty seconds. Take that time and connect with the writer you are, connect with the project you're working on, connect with the project you've not yet begun. Just the act of connecting with the spirit of your writing endeavor serves you in powerful ways.

Here's a suggestion:

You have no time to write today? If you have created a writing invocation or vision statement (see *Awakening Your Vision*, Chapter 11), take a few deep breaths to ground and relax yourself and speak those words of connection. If you have not yet done so, or even if you have, use this quick connecting exercise:

Close your eyes. Take a few deep breaths, in and out, in and out, breathing out whatever distractions surround you, whatever you were doing, thinking or saying before this moment.

Now, breathe in the essence of your creative self, the fire that *is* your creative self. Breathe in your book, your story or your project, if you have one. Breathe in your Muse. Breathe in the knowledge that you are a writer of power, strength and substance. See a flame or white light in your heart center. See it and breathe into it.

Connect with your Muse and assure it that you *will* sit down to write. Commit to a time. Commit to a place. Keep your appointment. Keep your commitment.

I Can't Write Until I...

Are you having a hard time getting to your writing? Does it always seem as though there's something (or ten somethings) that absolutely must be accomplished before you can start...and then the day is done, leaving you neither time nor energy to write? Do any of the following questions or phrases sound familiar?

- I'd better check my e-mail/voice mail...

- As soon as I [*insert task here*], I'll be able to write without worrying about it.

- I can't write on an empty stomach. I'd better get a snack.

- Let me just see who this is on the phone/at the door/in this new e-mail...

- That bathroom floor and [*insert anything here*] is disgusting. I'd better clean it first...

- Oh, I really need to call [*insert name here*] before I can start.

- I can't write until I [*insert distraction here*]...

- Let me just look that up on the Internet, then I'll be ready to write.

If you find yourself putting anything ahead of the blank page, you're not alone. Writers often have the cleanest windows, floors, fridges and toilets, the most up-to-date filing systems or the best record for returning calls or e-mails because, in the moment, just about any task seems more palatable than sitting down to write.

If you fall into that category, here are seven suggestions to minimize distraction and procrastination until you have completed your day's writing (or, at least, your first installment):

- Keep all Internet-related distractions out of sight and earshot until after you've written. Don't check your e-mail. Don't open your web browser. Turn off all e-mail, instant messaging and other notifiers that flash, beep or ping.

- Don't answer the phone or check voice mail. To avoid temptation, turn off your phone's ringer and your cell phone while you're writing and, if you use an answering machine, turn off the sound so that you can't hear who's calling. (Don't cheat by looking at the caller ID screen!)

- Don't open the morning paper or your mail. Don't check to see if they have arrived.

- Don't open your checkbook to pay bills.

- Don't start that book you've been meaning to read. Don't pick up that book you're a few pages from finishing.

- Don't pick up a sponge, mop or cleaning rag.

- Don't do *anything* unrelated to writing.

Again, perform no task or errand until you have written. If that has proven impossible, keep pen and paper or laptop by your bed and don't get up until you have written. That was how I got through the first hundred pages of my first draft of *The MoonQuest*.

Another benefit of making writing your first assignment of the day (other than getting it done!) is that you won't waste time during the rest of the day doing all the things you normally do to avoid writing.

Here's a suggestion:

Don't turn the page.
Stop reading.
Pick up your pen or touch your fingers to the keyboard.
Start writing. Now.

The Discipline of Your Heart

Mind discipline is rule-bound. It says: You will write for 62.5 minutes every day and produce 1,488 words at each sitting, each sitting commencing at precisely eight minutes past nine o'clock in the morning.

I exaggerate, of course. Yet much discipline is forced, rule-bound, punishing, joyless.

Heart discipline is different. It says that there is no optimal amount of time to spend at this or any writing session.

Heart discipline says, "Trust."

Trust that when you sit down, whenever you sit down, your Muse will answer your invitation (for your Muse is always with you). Trust that all you hear, including that it is either time to write or time to stop, is true. Trust that all the words that flow through you, be they five or five thousand, are the correct and appropriate ones for the moments in which you hear and record them.

Listen with your heart and discern. Listen with your heart and you will know, through practice, when it is time to start and when it is time to stop. You will know which words will ultimately go and which will stay. Listen to your vision for your work and hew to that. That is your discipline. That is your calling.

Let discipline be your discipleship to that vision, to that calling. That is what it means to be a writer from the heart, a writer of truth. That is what it means to be authentic — as a human being and as a writer. That is what it means to answer the call of your heart, to open to the voice of your Muse.

The Miracle of the Seed

It wasn't until I was 40 and living in the fertile farm country of Nova Scotia's Annapolis Valley that I experienced my first real garden. Frankly, it wasn't much of a garden — more a postage-stamp vegetable patch. Yet, tiny as it was, it was abundant with carrots, cucumbers, spinach, beans, tomatoes... and lettuce.

I still remember feeling like Jack-in-the-Beanstalk as I ripped open that first packet of lettuce seeds and held those magic specks in my palm before sprinkling them into the soil I had prepared.

With a plant, the evidence of creation is always visible. But when you sow from seed, you operate in the realm of faith. Once that seed is covered over, all you can do is trust, water and wait.

My miracle wasn't as dramatic as Jack's. It was a pale green frond, delicate against the rusty soil. Yet that dainty lettuce leaf was as magical to me as any giant beanstalk.

Much of the magic resided in the effortlessness of the enterprise. My sole task had been to drop the seeds into the ground, trust the dark mystery of Mother Earth and wait. When the time was right for both of us, that lettuce leaf pushed through the moist earth and cried out, "Here I am!"

Writing can be just as effortless. Buried in the dark mystery of our unconscious lie the seeds of books, stories, poems and articles. They, like my lettuce seeds, dwell in a universe beyond our visual, tactile, mind-centered world. Like my lettuce leaf, they emerge in *their* time, when the season is right, when the moment is ripe.

You believe your inner place is devoid of ideas? Trust in the darkness and silence of the earth. Trust in the fertility of your creative process. Trust in the seeds that lie dormant beneath the surface.

Trust that what needs to emerge will emerge when you create the conditions for that emergence, when you allow yourself the same space and silence you allow your seeds. Trust in the seasons of your writing, and the words will break through.

Today, take time to nurture the seeds now germinating in the dark earth of your being. Sit in the silence without poking and prodding, without questioning and analyzing. Be the seed you are and let the green shoots of your new growth develop and mature — into your awareness and onto the page.

Here's a suggestion:

Sometimes we're so busy doing, we never stop to be, to listen, to wait. Before you write today, give yourself five, ten or twenty minutes of nothingness, of silence. Sit in that silence as a seed sits in the soil. Breathe in the silence and breathe out your thoughts. Just be in the stillness... breathe in the stillness...listen...and wait.

When you're ready to write, notice any differences in how you feel. Are you more, or less, anxious, fearful, ready? When you start writing, notice any differences in what you're writing, how you're writing...the quality of the experience...the quantity of the output.

After you've written...

What did the silence feel like, produce, open you to? Write about that, too, today or another day, using either of these key phrases:

- "In the silence, I..."

- "Through the silence, I..."

Transitions

Ritual is not something to save for wedding ceremonies, communion rails or mealtime blessings. Ritual is a powerful device of transition, carrying you from one state of mind and consciousness to another.

It's about moving into an inner space where listening is possible. It's about shifting into the reality of openness — to receive, hear, trust and record.

That reality of openness is your natural state.

Of course, life gets in the way. That's okay. Ritual can carry us back to that place of connectedness and remind us of the totality of who we are. For who we are encompasses the spiritual as well as the physical, the being as well as the doing.

That place of connectedness is the place from which we create, the place from which we write. The more distracted and disconnected you feel during your day-to-day life, the more you may need the ritual of transition and the transition of ritual.

Devise your own rituals. Some may serve you for days, others for years. Some only once. Some may help only for certain projects. Some for certain parts of certain projects. Be flexible and find the rituals and transitions that work for you.

Remember, the words always come. They come because they are always present. Always. It is but for us to enter into that space of openness and receptivity where we can hear them.

Seven Tools for Transition

Pick the tools for transition that feel right for you in the moment. Feel free to adapt them. Feel free combine them. Don't hesitate to make them yours. Stay open and flexible to whatever will ease you into writing, recognizing that a particular practice may work for you once and never again.

1. Quick centering meditation

Sit down — at your desk, at your table, in your favorite chair, in your favorite part of the garden, on your favorite beach...wherever you feel comfortable, safe and inspired. Close your eyes, place your hands on your empty lap and breathe.

Breathe in and out slowly for ten breaths. Breathe in and out to a count of five or six or seven.

Feel your body relax. Feel each in-breath connect you to your creative source or your Muse and each out-breath flush all fear, doubt and anxiety from your system, flush all worldly concerns from your mind.

Focus on your heart and breathe into that space, into that fire, into that well of creativity. Breathe into the writing you intend to begin or continue. Breathe into the light and life and heart of it. Breathe into your heart connection with it. Breathe into your vision for it. Breathe into your truth.

Breathe in, breathe out and listen. If you find yourself ready to dive onto the blank page or screen before your ten breaths are up, go for it. This is not about rules. This is about getting you primed. Once you're primed, leap onto the page and let the words spill out of you.

2. Your breath

Breathe and breathe deeply — before you write, as you write and when you're done. It will open and keep alive your connection with your Muse, with Spirit, with your heart, with whatever you choose to call your creative source.

3. A special place

Choosing a special place in which to write can be part of ritual, particularly in the early stages of a project or as you're beginning to open more deeply to your creativity and the voice of your Muse.

If you cannot set aside an entire room, set aside a favorite chair or make a space on your desk that is free of clutter, where you can set out whatever keepsakes help keep you connected to your Muse and your writing. Perhaps it's an inspiring photo or art piece. Perhaps it's a favorite rock or crystal. Set it out. Light a candle, incense or an aromatherapy burner, if that helps. Create an atmosphere that is conducive to creation.

If you cannot use the same space each time you write, then carry those keepsakes with you that they may inspire you wherever and whenever you feel the call to write.

I wrote parts of this book in the car, parked at a lookout about two-thirds of the way up Kohala Mountain on the Big Island of Hawaii. With me most days was a portable altar: a hand-painted keepsake box filled with favorite crystals and inspirational art.

4. Writing invocation / vision statement

For me, the writing invocation I created for this book was often part of my gear-change from the outer to the inner, from mind-focus to Muse-focus. You'll read more about this, including how to create your own writing invocation or vision statement in *Awakening Your Vision,* Chapter 11.

5. Yoga / exercise

Relaxing the body relaxes the mind and removes your focus from the day's stresses and demands. Yoga, tai chi and other Eastern-inspired practices work well. But five or ten minutes of stretching or other exercises can achieve the same end.

Whatever else you do, focus on your neck, shoulders and eyes, all of which tighten easily when you're writing...or resisting. Shaking out your hands/wrists and feet/ankles can also be helpful, as are stretching exercises for your lower back, where we hold much of our resistance to change. Even an extended, full-mouth, tongue-stretching, jaw-loosening yawn (let a dog or cat be your model) can release much of the tension we often carry into the writing process.

6. Music

Music can set a mood, support a feeling, enhance your creativity. It can also block out unwanted sounds from the street or from elsewhere in your house.

Everyone is different and your music tastes may not be mine. When I work with music, I generally prefer something meditative that is not too melodic, something that doesn't intrude too deeply into my consciousness.

Among my favorites are Richard Shulman's *Light Music* and, with Samuel Welsh, his *Ascension Harmonics* (www.richheartmusic.com), *The Angels Gift* by Peter Sterling (www.harpmagic.com), anything by either Fiona Joy Hawkins (www.fionajoyhawkins.com) or Frederic Delarue (www.fredericdelarue.com), the out-of-print but still available *Pacific Shores: Sounds of the Surf* (Special Music Company) and the nature sounds generated by ChatterBlocker software (www.chatterblocker.com).

Find what works for you, and be flexible. What inspires you today may irritate you tomorrow.

7. Guided meditation

Create your own, record one of the meditations in this book or use a track from *The Voice of the Muse Companion CD* (see page 35). Whichever you choose, let its meditative energy carry you into a creative space.

Even if you're sitting in the car, waiting for your partner to finish work or your kids to finish school, you can pull out your favorite notebook, pop a CD into the player, take a few closed-eye breaths and allow yourself to be drawn into the magical realm of your Muse.

Distraction Happens

Distraction happens. You've been listening. You've been writing. Your connection to your heart and Muse has been strong, steady. The words have been pouring forth — swiftly, easily, joyfully.

Then, suddenly, the connection breaks up like a cell phone that's losing its signal.

Perhaps your child runs into the room. Perhaps your cat starts pulling papers off your desk. Perhaps your dog barks at the letter carrier. Perhaps you answer the phone instead of leaving it to voice mail. Or perhaps your stomach begins to growl so loudly it drowns out the voice of your Muse.

Distraction happens. Connections weaken, waver and snap. The tiniest slip in focus can disturb the flow. Some days my connection is so fragile that it severs when a fly buzzes around my head. Other days, I can work in a busy, buzzing café with no break in my focus and concentration.

Don't punish yourself. You will experience different connections on different days. This is normal and a function of many things: how much sleep you had last night, the last words you spoke to someone before you entered into this space and place, other things that are worrying you or weighing down your mind.

Some days you will be able to release all that with a single breath. Some days it will take many more breaths to release only a fraction of it. Either way is perfect.

Whenever the connection is threatened or too frail, focus on your breath and keep breathing. Always remember to breathe. Through your breath you can connect, listen and write under nearly any circumstance, in nearly any situation.

Keep breathing. That's where the connection lies.

If, in the end, you can't keep the connection alive? You've lost nothing. Accept the gift of what you have been able to write...and know more will flow, yet more freely, next time.

Here's a suggestion:

When distraction disrupts your flow, stop and sit with nothing but your breath. Focus on the air as it enters and leaves your lungs. Focus on your chest as it rises and falls. Focus on the silences as they ebb and flow. Take however long you need to breathe out the distractions and breathe in to your inner creative space, to the voice of your Muse, to the writer you are.

Consider, also, a meditative walk. Often a quiet break from desk, page or computer is all that's required to realign your focus and reconnect with the heart of your writing.

Put Away Your Journal

Put away your journal. I know you're frightened and anxious and want to clear that energy out of your system and into your journal. But how much time do you have for writing today? Do you have enough to contribute to your journal and start or finish that short story or poem, or continue with your novel or book project?

Today, I offer a new challenge. No, let's call it an opportunity: the opportunity to write through your anxiety — not by journaling, but by focusing on the work at hand.

This may seem impossible. It is not. It is possible to stay with your project, whatever it is, regardless of your state of being, regardless of your state of mind.

It's too easy to say, "I'm depressed. I'm anxious. I'm worried. Yes, I can write in my journal, but not on my current project."

You can hear the admonition coming, can't you? *Write on your project!* Period.

Don't let your journal become a distraction that keeps you from the work at hand. That's what happened to me for a while working on *The MoonQuest*. I was writing in my journal two, three, sometime four times a day but spending no time on the book.

When I realized what I was doing, I dropped the journaling completely until I was back in writing rhythm with *The MoonQuest*.

Use your journal as a tool, not a crutch. Use it to explore, not escape. Let the emotions you would release onto your journal pages express instead through your characters, your setting, your plot. Transform your anger into a scene, your fear into description, your anguish into dialogue.

Work on your project, if you have one...whatever it is. Do not let the cares of the moment stop you. They will, if you let them.

They need not. They are but distractions created by your fearful mind to divert you from your soul's work.

Allow your soul its imperative. Put aside your personality mind. Hold your focus and vision on all you desire to do, all your heart yearns for, all your Muse calls on you to express.

Your journal has its place. Discern what that place is for you from day to day. But place your primary focus on whatever song your soul would have you sing. Then sing that song onto the page. Sing it as loud as you can, with every ounce of strength you possess. Let that be your commitment — to yourself and to your Muse.

Here's a suggestion:

Next time you're feeling stressed and anxious — or joyful and exhilarated — don't reach for your journal. Reach instead for a blank sheet of paper and write about all you're feeling and experiencing — not as yourself but as a fictional character. Use the first person.

Here are some variations:

- Try varying the character's age, gender and other characteristics (also an effective way to fictionalize real people; see *Beyond the Physical*, page 193).

- Write the same feelings/experiences as different fictional characters.

- Begin a story using one or several of those characters.

Now Is the Time to Write / III

Now is the time to write. Now is the time to pick up your pen and touch its tip to your blank page. Now is the time to set that flashing cursor to work filling your empty screen.

See the words take shape out of nothingness. Watch the once-paralyzing void vanish in a flood of words, thoughts and images.

Whatever yearns to find its way onto the page will do so if you allow it the freedom to travel the shortest distance imaginable — from heart to hand to page.

Let your heart direct your hand.

What is it your heart cries out to express? What is it your heart has waited all these lifetimes to communicate, to share — first with you, then with others?

Close your eyes. For just a moment, close your eyes to the outside world that swirls so busily around you. Close your eyes and train your ears inward.

There is a word, one word, that your heart would have you hear. A single, simple word.

It is the first word that leaps to mind as you open, as you listen, as you hear. Perhaps it seems like nonsense, an irrelevance. Perhaps it is a nothing word to you, at this moment. Never mind. Now is the time to write, and now is the time to set that single, simple word onto the page.

Do it.

There. Now your page is no longer empty, your screen no longer blank.

How does that feel?

Don't tell me. Write it. Write your feelings on the page. Begin a new sentence and write, "I feel..." or "I fear..." or "I love..." or "I don't know..." Whatever you're feeling in this moment, commit it to paper. Commit to your writing. Commit to your emotions.

Do it. One sentence or one hundred. Place something on the page. Something. Anything.

Now, let one word lead to the next, then to another.

That's all writing is — one word leading to the next, then to another. Then to another.

And when you think you're done, stop thinking and keep writing. Just for a while longer, just to be sure you're not allowing some part of yourself to censor you or your words.

However long you've written, give yourself another ten minutes of writing on the Muse Stream, your pen never stopping, never ceasing its journey across the page, until the ten minutes have passed.

What happened?

Was there more or were you truly finished after stopping the first time? Some days there will be more, some days not.

Continuing past your first inclination to stop ensures that your work, not your fear, is in charge, that your heart, not your mind, is directing your writing. Continuing past your first inclination to stop may carry you to the true guts of your vignette, story, journal entry or poem...may carry you past a vignette or journal entry and into a poem or story.

Sometimes completion is completion. Yet sometimes the end we feel we have reached is the end of our comfort zone. So we stop. We believe we're done. We believe we've reached the perfect end-point.

By pushing on, you may go deeper. By not stopping after, say, fifteen minutes, but continuing to twenty or thirty, you may arrive in a place you weren't expecting.

Sometimes the first thousand words in a day's writing may have nothing to do with the project at hand. It's just what had to emerge to clear out what was in the way of continuing with that project with ease and clarity. It's a thousand words of anger, fear or frustration. So write through and past those emotions and discover the jewels they were hiding.

If you think you're done, continuing may push you to add more detail. Going on challenges you to keep adding what you might not want to, challenges you to go places you might prefer to avoid, takes you, perhaps, to the heart of the day's writing.

Go the extra distance. See where it takes you. See how it makes you feel. Trust that your words will always carry you where you need to go.

They will if you let them. They will if you let yourself. They will if you surrender to the wisdom of your heart, which is the wisdom of your art.

9.

Story

The universe is made of stories, not of atoms.

MURIEL RUKEYSER

All of us can sing the same song, and there will still be four billion different renditions.

ANNE LAMOTT

The Story Is There

The story is there. Your book exists. Your poem exists. Your song exists.

All you see, perhaps, is a blank page or empty screen — that virginal white sheet, that pixel blinking at you accusingly.

Nothing seems to be there. No words. No ideas. No stories. Not a hint of which key to press, which letter to form.

It scares you. It causes you to question whether you *are* a writer, whether you *can* answer the call to write that has been nagging at you for so long.

You wonder where all those stories that lie within you can be found, or if they truly exist. You wonder whether this "call to write," this sensing you have had forever, or only since you picked up this book, is real, has any basis, any grounding, any reality.

Because if it did, wouldn't you know what to write? Wouldn't you know how to start? Wouldn't you just sit down and let those words spill out of you until it was done?

The story is there. Learn to listen for it. Learn to listen to it. It *will* materialize...as first one word, then another; as first one sentence, then another; as first one page, then another.

It will. If you let it.

Let it.

The Ocean of Stories

There is an ocean of stories within you. There are unexplored depths in those waters of your unconscious mind.

Enter into them. Close your mind's eye to the danger and dive in. That is where the magic lies. That is where the beauty lies. That is where the truth lies.

You will not disappear or vanish in that ocean. You will not drown in those waves. You will be baptized and anointed. And you will emerge transformed.

You cannot control the changes that will have their way with you any more than you can control the story that passes onto the page when you write on the Muse Stream. But immersing yourself in that ocean of story will guarantee that you will be changed.

The act of telling a story, of setting it to paper, is a life-changing one. You must be open to the possibility of those changes, without knowing what they will be or how it will all work out when you first set pen to paper or fingers to keyboard.

You cannot control the outcome. You cannot know how the story will end. You cannot know what will happen around the next corner. All you can do is recognize the truth of this moment, of this feeling, of this word...and move on to the next from a place of trust.

Trust the story, and yourself — through each word and sentence — until your page is alive with the wonder of creation, until you are in wonder at the life of your creation.

Here's a suggestion:

Allow the ocean to be your Muse Stream as you dive in and write from this key phrase: "I swim in the ocean of story..."

Your Ocean of Stories

Guided Meditation #8

For optimal results, record this guided meditation and play it back for your own use, or have a friend read it to you. A version recorded by the author is also available on The Voice of the Muse Companion CD *(see page 35).*

Relax. Allow your breath to slow and deepen, slow and deepen, slow and deepen.

Close your eyes for a moment and picture an ocean. Any ocean. Anywhere. An ocean you have seen or visited, or one that resides only in your heart.

Whichever it is, see that ocean stretching out to the horizon, seemingly limitless in its scope. Feel its infinite nature, its infinite depth, its infinite breadth. Know that every story you have ever written or will write resides in that ocean, just as that ocean resides within you. Know that every story you have ever written or will write is as real and alive now as the sea life that thrives deep below the ocean surface of your imagining.

See yourself now in a boat on that ocean. Open ocean. A large boat or small. It doesn't matter as long as you feel safe, as long as you're comfortable, as long as it's your boat. Get a sense of that boat that now carries you, supports you, propels you forward. Feel the salt spray on your face. Feel the gentle swell of the ocean's ebb and flow. Ebb and flow. Ebb and flow.

Allow your breathing to align with that ebb and flow as you become one with this environment you are creating. This ocean. This boat. This sea of stories that stretches as far as the eye can see.

Farther.

If your boat is moving, allow it now to slow or stop. Anywhere. Anywhere at all. As long as you remain in open waters. Drop anchor or allow yourself to drift. It doesn't matter.

Now, in your hands is a net, a special net that scoops up not fish but stories. Stories from the vast undersea world that is the infinite reservoir of your creativity.

Take a deep breath now and cast your net into this sea of your creativity. Cast your net and let it fall where it falls, sinking wherever it sinks.

Take a few more breaths, allowing your net to settle. As your net sinks and settles, take a few more breaths, in and out, your breath following the ocean's swell. In and out. In and out. In and out.

Now it's time to raise your net. So do it. Raise your net and see what you have retrieved. What you have received.

Whatever it is is perfect. Perhaps what has emerged makes sense as a story. Perhaps it makes no sense to your conscious mind. It doesn't matter. Whatever it is is perfect in this moment. For this moment.

What have you retrieved from the ocean of story? From the depths of your creative waters?

See it. Feel it. Sense it. Know it. Fully.

And now, write it.

Everything Is Story

Everything is story. Everything. How you grew up is story. What you did on the way to the store is story. What you did to avoid sitting down and writing today is story. Whatever you do, whatever you breathe, whatever you speak, you are living and creating story.

Stories, as I've said, live in the air around you. The novel or short story that's been flitting and fluttering in and out of your awareness for — how long? That is story. The poem you have wanted to write about your first love, your current love, the birth of your child: These, too, are stories.

Everything we experience in this physical realm, everything we sense of other realms, everything we write — be it a letter to a friend, a journal entry, a nonfiction book or article, an epic novel or a vignette written on the Muse Stream — these all are stories.

Where do they come from? Nowhere and everywhere. They need not come from anywhere because they are always everywhere present. Be it a childhood memory or the piece of fiction that has yet to emerge into consciousness, your story already exists.

We talked a bit about that before. It bears repeating, for it's a revolutionary concept. So revolutionary that I will repeat it yet again. Your story — whatever it is — already exists. All your stories and all your books already exist in perfect, finished form. Simply travel to that realm we spoke of earlier — with an open heart, open eyes and an open mind — and write down the stories you discover there, the stories that speak to you...through the voice of your Muse.

Here's a suggestion:

Take a few moments to reconnect with your Muse, reentering that space you experienced in *Meet Your Muse* (page 36). Now, holding the energy of that experience, write on the Muse Stream from this phrase: "My story is..."

10.

Birthing Your Book...
Even if you don't know what it's about

There are three rules for writing a novel.
Unfortunately, no one knows what they are.

W. SOMERSET MAUGHAM

Novels are not necessarily written as the crow flies.

ALAN BENNETT

Your Book Is Waiting for You

Your book is waiting for you. It's waiting for you to notice it, waiting for you to catch up with it, waiting for you to surrender to it.

Perhaps you know you have a book in you. Perhaps you suspect it. Perhaps you know what it's about. Perhaps you don't.

It doesn't matter.

What matters is that you acknowledge that your Muse is trying to get your attention. What matters is that you open your heart and blank page to it. What matters is that you surrender.

I didn't know anything about a book called *The MoonQuest* when its words began to flow through me. I didn't know *The Voice of the Muse* was a book when these words you now read began pouring out of me. All I knew in both instances was that my Muse was calling me and that the only way to answer its call was to write.

As I wrote, the books took care of themselves.

One day's writing led to the next. One draft led to the next. One book led to the next.

Each day, draft and book drove my pen. My pen, in turn, drove me. My only job was to release all attachment to form, structure, content and outcome. My only job was to write and let the words go where they chose and create what was theirs to create.

As it turned out, they chose to create books I never planned to write.

The StarQuest was different. Even before *The MoonQuest* was finished, I knew *The StarQuest* was in me, waiting to emerge. I knew it was a book. I even knew a smidge of its story before I began.

So how did I begin?

The same way I begin every piece of writing: by beginning.

Whatever you know of your book and its content, you start every piece of writing the same way, with a single word. With a single letter. With a single pen stroke or key stroke.

Any word. Any letter. Any pen stroke or tap on the keyboard.

"In the beginning was the Word. And the Word was with God…"

Your first word also resides with God or your Muse or whatever creative source you acknowledge. So does your second and third and thirtieth and thirty-thousandth.

Whichever word gets you started is the right one. And that right one will inexorably lead you to the next and the next and the next. And the next…if you let it.

Ultimately, all those words will lead you through your book to its ending, an ending that has been waiting for you since the beginning of time. Of course it has, for your book has existed since the beginning of time, waiting patiently for you acknowledge it, open your heart to it and capture its essence in words on a page.

Are you ready to acknowledge it? Then pick up your pen or touch your fingers to the keyboard and free your first word onto the page.

You don't know what your book is about? If you listen it will tell you. If you surrender, it will guide you. If you let it, it will write itself.

Thirteen Rules for Birthing Your Book

1. **There are no rules.**

   This is the one rule that never changes. No matter what you're writing or revising, the only unqualified certainties are that flow is fluid, your creation is unique and your book writes its own rules. Truly, there is no universal right or wrong way. There is only your way, the way of your book.

2. **There's a difference between a good idea and the right idea.**

   A good idea for a book isn't always the right idea for your book. Be open to the right idea. Be open to the idea that not only sings to your soul but sings the song of your soul to the world. Be open to the idea that expresses your passion, the right idea that is uniquely yours. (See *The Right Idea*, page 121.)

3. **Forget everything you ever learned about writing.**

   Forget your grade school teacher who was a stickler for spelling and grammar. Forget your high school teacher who forced you to turn in an outline with your essay. Forget your college professor who forced you to write a certain way. Forget all the classmates or instructors who cruelly critiqued or ridiculed you. Forget all the writing manuals and instruction you've ever read (including, where appropriate, this one).

4. **Remember everything you ever learned about spirituality.**

   Be in the moment with each word, each page, each project. Set aside your will and surrender to the guiding voice of your Muse. Take neither praise nor criticism too seriously and hold your center as a writer and creator, regardless of what others say or suggest.

5. **Always use your discernment.**

   You know at a deep level what's right and what's wrong — with your writing, with your ideas, with your book. Trust that inner knowingness. Trust your heart. Trust your Muse. Trust your book.

6. Your book is smarter than you are.

Discard all assumptions that you know what your book is about, how it will end or how you will get to the end. Your book knows what it's about. Don't force your will onto it. Talk to it. Sit in the silence with it. Listen to it. Follow its lead.

6a. Your book is a trickster.

Your book may trick you into writing and discovering the unexpected, undesired, unwanted. This is good. Your book and your Muse see the higher perspective that you, sitting at your blank page or screen, cannot always see. Curse, mutter and resist if you must. Then surrender to your book's higher wisdom. It *is* smarter than you are. (See *Abandon Control*, page 50.)

7. Your book is older than you think.

Your book has been around a long time waiting for you to notice it, acknowledge it and muster up the courage to surrender to it. Your job is to do all those things and, in so doing, make manifest what has always existed. Your job is to allow the ideas of your heart to find expression through your mind. Like the God of Genesis, your job is to *let* creation happen.

8. You can make it easy or make it tough. Why make it tough?

It's easy to be overwhelmed by the thought of 300 blank pages waiting to be filled. It's easy to let the size and scope of a project paralyze you into inaction. Even as you hold a vision of the completed whole (see *Awakening Your Vision*, Chapter 11), break your book and its related tasks into manageable chunks. Create goals that are so easily achievable they're impossible not to meet. If that means saying you'll pen fifty words per writing session, that's fine. Set the goal and meet it.

It's important to build up a sense of the possible, to reassure yourself that your book is doable. As you meet your early goals, begin to stretch them and yourself, always keeping them clearly attainable.

Celebrate every accomplishment and achievement, however tiny. Avoid setting yourself up for failure. Each success will breed more confidence, each confidence, more success. And before you know it, your book will be done.

9. Write.

All it takes to write a book is to start, surrendering to one word after the next until you're done. (There's a reason why the word *surrender* appears seventy-seven times in this book!)

Many books and teachers insist that you know what you're writing about before you start. I say, just start. Your book knows the way. Let it guide you. Remember, no book can be birthed unless you first face a blank page or screen.

10. Relax. It's only your first draft.

You will have plenty of time in subsequent drafts to correct spelling, punctuation and grammar, to polish and hone, to do more research, to craft and to organize. Now is the time to surrender, to get the essence of your story — whatever that story is — onto the page.

11. It's all in order...even if it's not.

Like movies, which are rarely filmed in sequence, your first (or second) draft may not write itself in order. Let it come out as it comes out, knowing that your book's innate wisdom will determine the appropriate order when both you and it are ready.

12. It's perfect...even if it's not.

From your first draft to your last, what you're writing doesn't have to be perfect, can never be perfect. What it can be is the best expression of your heart and Muse you can allow onto the page. Let each word and each draft emerge as it emerges, surrendering to them as fully as you can. And when you sense completion, let your book go, freeing it into the world and freeing yourself to create anew.

13. There are no rules.

None. Not even these. Your page is blank for a reason. It's waiting for your creation, for the voice of your Muse to push, cajole, sweet-talk, threaten or charm you into filling it. One thing is certain: Unless or until you free the words that long to live through you onto the page, *you* won't be free — in your writing or in your life.

Do You Know What You Will Write Today?

Do you know what you will write today? I don't. I rarely knew what I would write about when I sat down to write this book.

Just as with *The MoonQuest*, I wrote this book without conscious plan, outline or control, without knowing what each day would bring or how it would contribute to the whole. All I could do was hold the vision and trust that somewhere beyond my immediate perspective, there existed purpose, form and structure.

Was it always easy? No.

Do I like to abandon control? No.

Does this method work? Always.

Both *The Voice of the Muse* and *The MoonQuest* were written precisely as I'm guiding you to write. *The StarQuest* writes itself the same way.

I have already described the genesis of *The Voice of the Muse*. *The MoonQuest* began for me in one of my workshops, during a writing exercise I chose to participate in. Later that night, I wrote on the Muse Stream from the final sentence of my workshop vignette...just to see where it would take me. Over the next year, I wrote most of the rest of the first draft in much the same way — rarely knowing from day to day (or word to word) where the story was going.

I tell you this so you will see and know and understand that it is possible to write anything of any length and in any genre by following the flow of the Muse Stream.

It is possible to take that leap of faith — be it into fiction or nonfiction, be it into a poem or into a heartfelt letter to a friend or lover. It is possible to take that leap of faith and let your heart be your safety net. For your heart *is* your safety net. Always.

Here's a suggestion:

Go back to what you wrote yesterday or the day before. Take the final sentence of that piece — whatever it was — and use it as today's key phrase. Perhaps, like *The MoonQuest* was for me, it will be a continuation. Perhaps it will be the start of something new. Surrender to the journey and see where it takes you.

If you're working on a book, try beginning each day's writing by writing on the Muse Stream from the previous day's final sentence. Abandon control and let the book's innate wisdom guide you forward.

11.

Awakening Your Vision

Let the eagle be your guide to go farther
than you can see.

MICMAC SAYING

You have to leave the city of your comfort
and go into the wilderness
of your intuition.

ALAN ALDA

What's Your Vision?

Do you know who you are as a writer? Do you have a vision for your writing? Do you have a vision for the project you're working on? For the project you have barely begun to conceive?

Connecting with and holding a vision for yourself as a writer and for your work will help you more easily move into writing and hold the energy of your creation through the entire process of conception, creation, revision and release.

One way to hold that vision is by creating a writing invocation or vision statement that propels you into the energy of your day's writing. It can be as short as a sentence or as long as a page. It can speak in general terms about your role as a writer or in specific terms about a particular book, poem, article, song or story — whether you already know what it is or just that you're called to write it.

I used both an invocation and vision statement for this book. Together they formed part of the ritual that awakened me to my Muse, activated my inner writing space and ensured that all I wrote hewed as closely as possible to the book's true essence.

Invocations and vision statements are not fixed in stone. As this book progressed, as I matured through the writing of it, I continued to refine both my invocation and vision statement.

On the next pages you'll find my invocation and vision statement for *The Voice of the Muse*, as well as *Vision Quest*, a two-part guided meditation to help you connect with your vision and create your own invocation and vision statement.

Writing Invocation for The Voice of the Muse

I, Mark David Gerson, open my heart and mind to the transformative wisdom that lies within me.

I activate the divine connection between my heart, mind and hand, allowing the words, sentences and paragraphs of *The Voice of the Muse* to flow freely onto the page.

I invoke my visionary, creative and alchemical power to bring this book, already completed and published in other realms, into the physical in its whole, complete and perfect state.

I suspend and dissolve any and all judgment, criticism, fear, self-pity and self-hatred that might stand in the way of initiating and completing this transformation.

I choose for *The Voice of the Muse* to answer *my* call to write — to help transform me and others through the words and energy that are mine alone to transmit.

I honor that call by moving forward, free of all self-imposed encumbrances. The words flow freely through me and onto the page, in their most perfect and transformative form.

The flow is reinitiated each time I speak these words.

Let the flow begin, let the Muse Stream of words and ideas run freely through me that I may be immersed in its waters and that those waters may flow out into the world, anointing and transforming all who touch and are touched by them, beginning with me.

Let the flow begin. Now.

Vision Statement for The Voice of the Muse

The Voice of the Muse: Answering the Call to Write is about freedom —
freedom to grow, freedom to create, freedom to write. Through a dynamic
blend of motivational essays, inspiring meditations and practical exercises,
it nourishes, nurtures and reassures its readers, inspiring them to open their
hearts, expand their minds and experience, with ease, a full, creative life.

Vision Quest

Guided Meditation #9

For optimal results, record this guided meditation and play it back for your own use, or have a friend read it to you. A version recorded by the author is also available on The Voice of the Muse Companion CD *(see page 35).*

Allow at least 45 minutes to complete both parts of this exercise.

Part 1 / Imaging Your Work

Relax. Close your eyes. Let your hands fall to your lap if you're sitting, to your abdomen if you're lying down. Breathe...deeply...in and out...in and out...in and out.

If you are setting off on this journey any later than first thing in the morning, run back over your day on fast-forward, and every time you get to something that was harsh or jarring, be it a thought, word or action — yours or someone else's — breathe in deeply and blow it out. As fully and noisily as you dare. As many times as you need to. Just blow it out.

And any moment that was particularly wonderful, breathe it in deeply and reconnect with the energy of that.

Continue to breathe, deeply, and focus on your eyes. If you wear glasses or contacts, imagine, for a moment, perfect vision without them. Imagine unassisted clarity without correction.

Breathe into that.

See white light around your eyes and your third eye, that chakra or energy center that lies between your eyebrows and above the bridge of your nose. See that white light cleaning, clearing and cleansing any blurriness, fuzziness, distortion. Feel all veils being pulled away, one by one by one by one. And as each veil dissolves, your vision becomes clearer and clearer and clearer.

Now, without removing all your attention from your eyes, move some of your focus to your heart. Be aware of the veils that surround your heart, whatever form they take. Just be aware of them. Don't judge them.

Now, taking a deep breath, let the outermost veil fall away. Just feel it fall away and dissolve. And when you breathe in again, notice that your heart feels lighter and freer and clearer.

And as you breathe in again, another veil falls away. And another. And another.

Feel how much lighter your heart feels, how much freer your heart feels.

It's okay if it feels a bit scary. Just feel what you feel. Know that you are safe.

Keep breathing and feel yourself grow lighter and freer, lighter and freer, as you move closer to the heart of the matter and closer to who you are as the writer you are.

And what a wondrous place that is.

Once more, breathe in, and if there is another veil there, breathe it away. And the next. And the next. And the next, until all that remains is a brilliant light, no longer veiled and dimmed, in your heart. Breathe into that and feel it.

Now, let the light from your eyes and the light from your heart connect in a ring of light that circulates energy from eyes to heart and around again. Either clockwise or counterclockwise. It doesn't matter. Whichever way it happens is perfect for you. However the light moves for you, allow yourself to sense it, to feel it. Your vision and your heart as one.

Now, see a second ring of light, moving in the opposite direction from the first, this time connecting your heart to the hands resting on your lap or abdomen. Again, be aware of the circular motion of this circulating energy. Around and around. A constant and consistent river of radiance.

Connect the two rings and you now have a figure eight or infinity symbol within you, as this inner light arcs from eyes to heart...heart to hands...hands to heart...heart back to eyes. And again. And again. And again, creating an infinite, luminous flow with your heart as its center.

As the energy circulates through that figure eight, be aware of the light pulsing in the topmost tips of your fingers, the hands with which you create, the hands that form part of the channel that brings your worlds into reality. Perhaps you feel the pulsing. Perhaps you don't. Whatever you feel physically, know that the energy is there, the light is there. The creative power is there — in your fingers, in your hands, in your eyes and in your heart, as the flow continues.

Sit with that flow for a few moments, feeling yourself immersed in its river of light and in the creative power that is moving through you.

Now, move your focus away from the infinity symbol and back to your eyes, your heart and your hands. Let a beam of light radiate out from your eyes, another beam of light from your heart and a third beam of light from your hands — all meeting at a point in front of you, in front of your heart.

That point in front of you, connected to you by all that light, is your work as a writer.

Perhaps it's your body of work. Perhaps it's a particular piece of work. Or a single aspect of your work. It doesn't matter. Whatever feels right in this moment, let that be whatever it is in this moment.

So your work stands separate from you but connected to you, in that space where all the columns of light meet just in front of you, in front of your heart.

There is your writing.

I'm going to ask you some questions about your writing. I want you to allow the first answer that comes to mind to be *the* answer. And I want you to know that you will remember it long enough to put it on paper, if that's where it needs to go.

So, focusing the beams of light that travel from your heart, eyes and hands and onto that writing space in front of you...

- If your writing were a color, what color would it be? Just let the color come. Note it. Don't judge or analyze it. Be with it. Know that in this moment, that color represents your writing. Be with that color for a few breaths.

- Now, your writing is a space, shape or image. What is that space, shape or image? Again, don't judge or analyze. Let it be what it is. See it if you can. Note it. Know that this, too, you will remember long enough to write down or draw, if appropriate.

- Now, your writing is a sound. Music, perhaps. What kind of sound, what kind of music is it, for you, in this moment? Breathe into that sound. Be part of it and one with it. Let it surround you and enfold you, filling you with its melodies and harmonies, with its simplicity or complexity. That sound, however it is, whatever it is, is part of you. You will remember that too, when and if it comes time to put it to paper...or sing it, if that is how you choose to express it.

- Now, use your sense of smell. What does that tell you about your writing, about who you are as a writer? Is it a sweet smell? A smell that reminds you of something? Again, just be aware of it, and let it be.

- One more sense: What would your writing taste like, if you could taste it? Perhaps there's a particular food or type of food. Maybe it's a chocolate sundae, rich and creamy. Maybe it's comfort food — mashed potatoes and gravy. Maybe it's fresh, baked bread. Maybe it's a juicy pineapple. Maybe it's sweet and flowing like honey. Maybe it's spicy...tangy...tart. Let it be what it is. Acknowledge it. Be with it.

Now, go deeper still and let one word emerge that captures the spirit and essence of your work. Let it be the first word that comes, whatever it is. Don't judge it, don't analyze it. Don't second-guess.

If it makes no sense to your conscious mind, perhaps that's just as well. Let it be.

Now, staying in this meditative space that you're in, pause the recording and jot down some notes about what you experienced — the color, the smell, the taste, the shape, the word...particularly the word.

Or take the word that just came to you and write on the Muse Stream from the phrase, "My writing [or *name of project*] is [*insert your word*]..."

When you're done, put your pen down and, without reading what you've written, restart the recording, close your eyes and continue with Part 2 of the meditation.

Part 2 of this meditation begins on the next page.

Reconnect with that energy, that space. With that triangle, that pyramid of light. Again, begin to feel the light connecting your eyes and heart and hands with your work, your work as the writer you are.

Now that you've experienced your writing from each of your senses, move your directed focus away from those specific senses.

Stand above them. Get an overview of all that you experienced, all the different connections you felt with your writing through sensing your writing.

From that vantage point, look down at that space in front of you where you and your writing come together, and breathe into that space for a few breaths.

Feel the fullness of it and the vastness of it. The specifics of it, too. Feel all of it. Be all of it. Know all of it for the first time, again.

Feel, too, your connection with that part of you that is the writer and the writing and the work. Feel it and breathe into it. Breathe deeply into it.

Now, answer these questions...

- What is it that, deep inside of you, you want to convey through your work? First answer. No thinking about it. Let the answer come freely.

- What is it you want people to experience through your work? Again, go with whatever comes up first. Don't censor. Don't judge.

- What do you want people to experience of *you* through your work?

- What do you want people to experience of *themselves* through your work?

Open your eyes, again pause the recording and jot down your answers to some of those questions, to whichever questions were answered.

Remember not to judge or analyze. Just record your experiences, the answers you've received.

Stay in a meditative space and, when you're done, restart the recording.

～✒︎～

Turn to a fresh sheet of paper. At the top of the page, write: "I, *your name*, am a writer. Through my writing [*or the name of a work*], I..."

From that opening, write on the Muse Stream, letting what follows be as long or as short as it needs to be.

When you're done, sit quietly in the energy of that for a few minutes before reading it aloud. Feel free to revisit and revise this statement or series of statements as you, your project and your writing mature.

12.

Breathing Light and Life into Your Writing

Although much of this section focuses on fiction, you can
easily adapt its ideas and techniques
to other types of writing.

Every writer must choose between safety and invention.

ALLEGRA GOODMAN

*Better than a thousand useless words is one
single word that gives peace.*

THE DHAMMAPADA

Free Your Characters. Free Your Story.

"God said, 'Let there be light,' and there was light. ..."

Your act of creation is like God's in Genesis, an act of allowance, of letting... of surrender. Surrender to the story that calls to be written, surrender to how it calls to be written, surrender to the lives your characters choose to live. For, if you're writing fiction, those lives *are* your story.

Just as the Creator in most religious and spiritual traditions allows you the free will to live your imperative and forge your story through the living of it, your call is to allow the beings who leap from your heart, mind and vision the same freedom. Gently guide when necessary, but allow them — and yourself — to experience their story as it writes itself onto the page.

Your job as creator is to *let* your characters and their story emerge from the formless void and to breathe life into them so that they — and you — can experience all they have come onto your page to live.

Let there be light...and there will be.

Be Specific

Imagine you're painting a picture. What would you want your reader to see and experience? Specifics bring your reader more fully into that picture, into your story, into an experience that becomes theirs.

Use all your senses — spiritual as well as physical — to describe your people and places, your subjects and objects. You might want to adapt the *Vision Quest* meditations (page 174) for this purpose.

What are the colors — of eyes, cars, sunsets, buildings, moods? Are there original ways you can express those colors? By using metaphor? A different point of view? A child's perspective?

Name your birds, streets, characters, towns, countries.

What's the model of the car? The year? Is the interior cloth or leather? New-looking or worn? Pristine or littered with greasy McDonald's cartons?

Describe foods, settings, backgrounds.

What are the smells and sounds? The textures? The memories they evoke?

Open to new ways of relating these to your reader. What do they remind you of? Who do they remind you of?

As in all aspects of your writing, stay in balance. Over-description and mega-detail can be as off-putting as not enough. Allow what you paint to most resemble an Impressionist painting — just enough color and detail to allow your readers to "connect the dots," but not so hyperreal that it overwhelms them.

Know Your People. Know Your Places.

Discover as much as you can about your settings and characters (or subjects, if you're writing biography or profile).

With people, know not only their physical attributes but their secrets and dreams. Know not only the color of their eyes but the quality of the fire behind those eyes. Know what happened in their lives before you entered the scene, before their recorded story begins. Know what shaped them, what excites them, what scares them. Know them as well as — better, perhaps, than — you know yourself and, in that knowing, they will leap off the page with full humanity.

With places, know not only how they look but how they feel. Know not only what's visible but what's invisible. Know what's ordinary and extraordinary about them. Use all your senses to discover and describe their sounds, smells and textures. Their essence and spirit. Their character.

Here are six ways to deepen your knowledge of people and places.

1. Visualization

Close your eyes and get into a meditative space. Envision yourself in a safe, creative place and let your character or characters take shape. Have them guide you through their day, their home, their life. Notice how they dress, how they wear their hair, how they walk, how they talk. Let them show you who they are and how they live. Let them show you who they were and where they came from. Let them show you who they will be and how they expect to get there. Watch them relate to others. See them as they experience joy. Eavesdrop on them in an intimate moment. Witness their response to a crisis.

With story or article settings, see yourself walking or driving through them, floating above them, looking up from beneath them. How else can you view them? Note the differences each perspective offers you. Explore not only the seen but the unseen, the past and possible future as well as the present. Visit the attractive and desirable, but also check out the unattractive and seamy. See it all, employing all your senses, physical as well as spiritual and intuitive.

2. Dialogue

With paper and pen or keyboard and monitor at hand, get into a meditative space and enter into a written conversation with your character. Ask questions...and wait for answers. Let your characters tell you who, what and why they are...how they are feeling, and why. You can do the same with place...even with physical objects. For they, too, can be living, sentient characters in your story.

After a few drafts of *The MoonQuest*, three of my four main characters didn't feel fully formed. I dialogued with each of them in turn and discovered things I hadn't known, including some I didn't want to know. Those dialogues became scenes that merged seamlessly into the narrative, as if the story had been waiting for them...and me.

3. Imagery

Give your senses free reign. Ask not only what your character looks like, but what he sounds like, what she smells like, what his skin feels like. If your character were a taste or a flavor, what would that be? If your character were an animal or a bird, which animal or bird would she be? If he were a color or shape, which would he be?

Use imagery, too, to deepen your sense of place, describing it in ways that call not only on sight, sound, taste, touch and smell but on all sensory possibilities, including the numinous and otherwordly.

Remember to use your intuitive and visionary abilities — we all have them — to tune into the story of his life, the life of her story...to tune into the spirit and essence of each place.

5. Point of view

Write as your character, in first person and on the Muse Stream, from his or her point of view. For example, "My name is..." or "I love to..." or "When I look in the mirror, I see..." Or write on the Muse Stream in third person using your character's name as a key word. If you don't yet know her name, write "This character's name is..." You can also write on the Muse Stream from any attribute or attributes. For example, "Joanne's hair is..." or "Jack's favorite pastime is..." or "When Frieda meets a new person, she..."

To learn more about how your characters relate to their family, friends and environment, write about them from the point of view of other characters. Write about them, too, from the perspective of the places they work, visit or inhabit.

If your settings have character-like significance, explore them in a similar fashion. "I am John's house. When he's home, I..." "I am the New York of Janet and her story. I..." Write about the places from the point of view of different characters for a fuller sense of their depth and relevance.

6. Lists

Create a checklist of attributes and characteristics, or use *All About People* or *All About Place* on the following pages. From a place of openness and surrender, run through each attribute and characteristic and allow its specifics to emerge...easily. As in all your writing, go with first thoughts and don't second-guess what emerges.

If you start with the lists I've created, feel free to revise them, eliminating characteristics that aren't relevant and adding ones better tailored to your story. Fashion additional lists for other aspects of your story. Experiment by writing on the Muse Stream from any responses you get.

All About People

- Gender
- Name
- Age
- Weight
- Height
- Frame
- Eye color
- Marital status
- Hair color (original? dyed?), style, length
- Facial hair
- Figure and body type
- Vision (nearsighted, farsighted, glasses, contacts)
- Gait (how your character walks)
- Posture
- Voice/manner (soft, grating, blustery)
- Preferred manner of dress
- What your character normally wears, if different
- Job(s)
- Schooling
- Parents' names
- Children's names/ages
- Siblings' names/ages
- Ethnic background
- Family
- Greatest wish/desire

- Greatest regret
- Greatest fear
- Best dream already fulfilled
- Worst nightmare
- Favorite color
- Favorite music
- Favorite food
- Allergies
- Hobbies
- Unusual skills
- Unusual traits
- Mannerisms
- Scars
- Phobias
- Eccentricities
- Favorite beverage, how your character takes coffee/tea
- Favorite snack food
- Favorite restaurant
- Favorite pastime
- Preferred type of reading, movie, etc.
- Punctuality (never/always late, never/always early, never/always on time)
- Pets
- Relationship with men
- Relationship with women
- Relationship with children
- Relationship with animals
- Relationship with self
- Favorite art
- Favorite expression

All About Place

Time
- Time of day
- Season
- Time of year
- Era

Pace of life
- Fast/slow
- Urban/rural
- Rushed/lazy

Natural geography
- Flat/hilly/mountainous
- Barren/lush
- Desert/ocean
- Rivers/lakes

Natural environment
- Trees
- Flowers
- Grasses
- Shrubbery
- Other plantings
- Soil color/type
- Lushness/sparseness/health

Weather and climate
- Type/quantity/quality of wind, rain, clouds, sun, snow, fog
- Aridity/humidity
- Temperature

Urban geography

- Real/imaginary/mythical
- Country
- Region
- City/town/village
- Street/road

Built environment

- House/buildings
- Neighboring structures
- Relationship between structures
- Interiors/exteriors
- Signs
- Street architecture (benches, lampposts, trash cans, etc.)

Vehicles

- Cars
- Trucks
- Bicycles
- Pushcarts
- Motorcycles
- Buses
- Horse-drawn vehicles
- Baby carriages/strollers

Indoor environment

- Plants
- Flowers
- Wall hangings
- Furnishings
- Floor coverings
- Light/lamps (bright or dim?)
- New/worn
- Conservative/avant-garde/eccentric
- Ordered/disordered
- Matching/mishmash

Indoor climate

- Comfortable/uncomfortable (how?)
- Aridity/humidity
- Temperature

People and animals   (see also *All About People*)

- Ages
- Types
- Sizes
- Activities

Miscellaneous

- Normal v. unusual
- Visible v. invisible
- Public v. secret
- Numinous/supernatural
- Atmosphere

Dominant sensory stimuli

- Colors
- Tastes
- Smells
- Sounds
- Textures
- Spirit

Secondary/subtle sensory stimuli

- Colors
- Tastes
- Smells
- Sounds
- Textures
- Spirit

Beyond the Physical

Don't restrict yourself to the physical. You want his vital statistics, of course. You also want to know her goals and desires, current and past occupations, fears and frustrations, education, opinions and prejudices. You want to know where, how and with whom he lives...where, how and with whom she loves. You want to know her hobbies and interests, mannerisms and manner of dress. You want to know his secrets. You want to know her fantasies.

You want to know what the scene looks like, but also what it feels like — when your characters are present, but also when they're absent.

You want to know everything!

Use all your senses and employ all your curiosity. Write down all you see and experience as you spend time with your people and places.

Keep your mind and heart open to all you perceive and receive, particularly anything that shocks, frightens, irritates or embarrasses them...or you. Through your discernment, you will know what feels right, what feels true. Go with that, not with what your second-thoughts censor would have you do. Let your people and places speak to you. For only then can they speak to your readers.

Not everything you discover will find its way into the final manuscript, nor should it. But the depth of your knowledge will inform and enliven every word and scene you write.

At the same time, don't be compulsive, and don't allow your list-making to be an excuse not to write!

Here's a suggestion:

Often characters spring from a story you have begun to write. Sometimes, though, a character enters your consciousness to spark a new story. Be open to this possibility. When you have no story in progress, let a character into your life — through meditation, visualization, dialogue or the Muse Stream, through dream or by fictionalizing a real person — and discover the story that awaits you.

Fictionalize a real person by changing a few key characteristics: age, gender, name, occupation, race, height. You'll be amazed at how different from your model the resulting character becomes.

Take Your Time

In the Bible, God created heaven and earth in six days. You're not working to the same deadline.

Let your world and its inhabitants take all the time they need to develop, mature and reveal themselves to you.

Remember, creation is a process. Don't feel you must know every last character detail before you begin your story. Don't let the little you think you know about your character or characters, settings or plots overwhelm you and prevent you from writing.

Begin your story. Let the characters emerge. They will reveal themselves to you in the writing. Use the concepts and techniques in this section to fill any gaps you perceive as you proceed with your first draft or subsequent drafts. Use them as breaks from storytelling. Use them between drafts. Use them as tools for enrichment. Don't obsess or allow yourself to feel inadequate.

Discover what you can and let the rest go. Do your best, take your time... and keep writing!

13.

After You've Written

Half my life is an act of revision.

JOHN IRVING

*Have patience toward all that is unsolved
in your heart and try to love the
questions themselves.*

RAINER MARIA RILKE

Gold Stars

"What's the use?" you ask, now that you have written. "What's the use of this story that means nothing, goes nowhere, won't sell? What's the use of these words that form no cogent whole, make no sense, are just too weird? Who will read this, buy this, publish this? Why did I bother?"

You're asking the wrong questions.

The value of your writing has little to do with your words and their form, nothing to do with another's opinion. It has everything to do with you.

Writing anything serves *your* growth, *your* development, *your* transformation. Thus everything you create has utility. Every word that finds its way onto the page, every draft that finds its way into the trash can, every manuscript that fails to find a publisher — immediately or ever — has value. Its existence is proof of that value.

If questions must be asked when the writing is done, try "How did I perform this miracle? How can I celebrate my creatorship? How do I reward my courage?"

When your final word touches down on the page, forget recrimination and second-guessing. Pay no attention to what others think. Pay no attention to what you think. Cancel all comparisons.

Comparison is nothing more than an excuse to put yourself down. "Oh," you say, "I could never write like that." Well, you don't have to write like that. Somebody already has.

The world isn't waiting for another Shakespeare, another Hemingway, another Atwood, another Didion. The world waits for you. You and your unique expression. You and your words. You and your story.

Even if the world never reads that story, you have created it. And having created it, you will never be the same.

Acknowledge your creation. Celebrate your achievement. Energize your accomplishment. Give yourself a gold star.

Here's a suggestion:

You've written. Now celebrate. Reward yourself. Do something extra-special for you that validates your achievement.

Too often, we direct all our attention to what remains *un*accomplished, ignoring the great distances we have already travelled.

Whenever you write, you travel great distances. Recognize that. Focus energy on your accomplishment. Acknowledge your abundance of words not your lack of pages. Grade-school children get gold stars when they do well. If you have written today, what will your gold star be?

Remember to honor yourself, always, for meeting the challenge... whatever it is.

Breathe in Discernment

Suspend judgment. Expel it altogether. Breathe it out with one forced-air breath and let it evaporate, dissipate and disappear.

Now, breathe in discernment. Discern what is powerful about your writing and what is weak. Discern what is strong and what needs work in your writing.

Discernment is a delicate tool. Judgment is a blunt hammer, a judge's gavel. It knocks you out with a "Guilty" or spares you with an "Innocent." You need subtler skills, more refined tools.

Discernment is a marriage of intuition and intellect, a blend of right and left brain, a meld of heart and mind, a whole-body approach to writing and to life.

There is no good or bad, right or wrong, righteous or evil, in discernment. There is inner knowingness, a weighing of merits, a gentle, loving approach.

There is no hanging discerner as there is a hanging judge. No one will be put to death. No one will be arrested. No one will be harmed in any way. There is no need for harm when discernment is at play. There is no black and white. There is no comparison. There is no absolute morality.

Judgment is about absolutes, and there are none in a place of the heart. There are no absolutes where love rules.

Yes, you are called to love your work. You are called to love it in the same way you love your child. Both are creations of the heart.

You do not judge your child. You weigh his or her behavior with discernment. You do not weigh it with judgment.

Your child needs to be nurtured, cared for and loved. So does your work. Your child needs correction, lovingly applied. So does your work. Your child is a creation of the heart. So is your work. Next time you would slash your work, ask yourself: Would I treat a child this way, no matter how badly she or he had behaved?

Your work is your child, a living, breathing entity — sentient, even. Love it, nurture it. Feed it. Give it its due time and attention. When it has matured, not to perfection but to completion, let it go and set it free that it might have its own life and free you to move on.

Love your work. Judge nothing about it. Allow your innermost wisdom and light — your discernment — to tell you when what you are writing is true and faithful to your vision and heart and when it is not.

When it is not, correct and change it without punishment, without shame and without false pride. Correct it with mercy, with forgiveness, with love. (See *The Heartful Art of re-Vision*, next page.)

Find the right vision for yourself and your work. Stay on the path of your vision as best as you can. And when you stray, have the mercy to forgive and the forgiveness to be merciful.

You are not your work. Your work is an extension and expression of you. Let it be that. Do not judge it. Do not judge the voice. Do not judge the words. Do not judge any small or large part of it. Discern the truth and that truth will always keep you free.

Here's a suggestion:

Take something you've written recently, or write something new for this exercise, and read it — no pen in hand — from a place of discernment, love and respect. No judgment. No criticism. Read it, rather, from a place of openheartedness, self-nurturing, mercy and forgiveness.

How does it feel to approach your work this way? How is it different from other times you've reread you work? How is it the same? How will it be different next time?

The Heartful Art of re-Vision

See the editing process as one of *re*-vision — revisiting the original vision you had for your work and putting all your heart, art and skill into aligning what's on paper with that vision.

As you move through your piece — whatever it is, whatever its length — see yourself as a jeweler, delicately etching your rough stone into the gem that reflects the vision your heart has conceived and received, then lovingly polishing it until you achieve the look and texture you desire.

Your vision is the light force of your work, the life force of your work. It's the spirit that is its essence, the breath that keeps it alive. Your vision is your dream for your work, the expression of your intention. It's what guides it, drives it and propels it — from conception to completion.

The more deeply you stay connected to that vision — however broadly or specifically you have drawn it — the more completely the finished piece will remain true to that life force, that dream, that intention. And the truer you will be to the work that has called upon you to commit it to paper and breathe life into it.

Here's a suggestion:

If you haven't already done so, create a vision statement for your piece of writing. It can be as simple as getting into a meditative space and writing on the Muse Stream from the phrase, "My vision for [*name of work*] is..." Or allow your work to speak about itself, writing on the Muse Stream from a phrase like, "I am [*name of work*]. I am about..." Or use the *Vision Quest* meditations (page 174).

Whatever your choice, allow to come whatever comes, whether it speaks in metaphor, in general terms or with the most specific of detail. The length doesn't matter. The form and language don't matter. Your conscious mind's understanding of what you have written doesn't matter.

What matters is that, at some level, you and your creation sing the same song and that that harmony supports you not only as you write but as you refine and enrich your original draft.

Revisit Your Vision. Revisit Your Work.

Before you begin your first revision, reread your vision statement — aloud, if possible. The sound of your voice will add power and resonance to your intent.

Don't just read it. Connect with it and, through it, connect with your work.

Hold this vision in your heart through each draft and each revision. Hold this vision when you send the final version out into the world. Hold this vision when you receive feedback or criticism. This vision will always keep you centered and aligned with the true heart of your work.

Once you have revisited your vision, it's time to revisit your work.

First Read-Through

The first step is to read it all the way through, aloud if practical, holding your vision in your heart and leaving aside doubt and self-criticism. Resist the temptation to make major changes. Resist the temptation to make any changes. Try reading with no pen in hand. Read for spirit, for an overview. Read in the same flow you wrote it. Read without judgment. Read for fun.

Second Read-Through

With pen or pencil in hand, make general notes about things that need changing. Circle inappropriate words or images. Note inconsistencies. Continue to resist the temptation to make substantive changes.

Subsequent Read-Throughs

Begin making the changes referred to in your notes and those suggested in *Eighteen Rules for Revising Your Work* (next page). Don't try to fix everything on the same read-through. Continue to hold your vision in your heart as you align your work with its highest expression.

Eighteen Rules for Revising Your Work

1. There are no rules.

By now, you should know that this is the only rule that counts! There is no right way to revise, other than to respect your work and yourself as its creator.

2. Be true to your vision.

Are there words, phrases or scenes that detract from the essence of the work, that weaken your theme, that don't illuminate your vision? Consider cutting them. Or rework them so that they strengthen your vision.

3. Be specific.

What make and color is the car? What does it smell like? What kind of flowers are in the bouquet? What shapes are the clouds? Is the grass clipped or unruly? Is it green or brown? (Reread *Be Specific*, page 184.)

4. Use imagery.

What do things smell and taste like? What do they sound like? What is their texture? Cross senses for more powerful imagery. Ask what the wind tastes like, what the earth sounds like…what your character's face feels like, what the town smells like, what your heartbeat looks like. Adapt *Vision Quest* (page 174) to connect with the sensory power of your piece.

5. Paint word pictures that draw on related images.

For the title of this rule, I chose words like "paint," "pictures" and "draw" to create and reinforce a particular idea. Would it have been as strong had I written, "Use word pictures that tap into related images"? The power of your imagery can increase when you build on related images to describe something. This is particularly true in poetry, but it works equally well in prose — fiction or nonfiction. When one image in the series breaks from the theme, you weaken your overall picture. As with any other tool, be careful not to overdo it.

6. Let your language sing.

Be aware of the rhythm of your language, the music of your words. Reading aloud helps. Are you varying your sentence structure? Do the type and length of your sentences support the scene and its mood? A series of short, simple sentences, for example, can build suspense. Longer sentences slow the reader down to a more leisurely pace. Know the effect you want and how best to achieve it.

7. Use powerful nouns and verbs.

Adjectives and adverbs can be crutches that hold up weak nouns and verbs. Find evocative verbs and nouns that stand on their own power and kick away those crutches. Adverbs and adjectives are valuable tools. They are more valuable when coupled with forceful verbs and nouns. Make friends with a good thesaurus.

8. Keep it simple.

Be simple. Be direct. Avoid four- or five-syllable words when words of one or two syllables work as well. In simplicity lies power. Don't overwhelm your reader with flowery excess. Don't show off.

9. Cut the fat.

Have you used two or three words — or sentences — where one would do? Keep your work lean and trim. Say more with less. Look for words like "very," "actually," "really" and "quite." ~~More~~ often ~~than not, actually,~~ they are ~~really quite~~ unnecessary.

10. Fill in the gaps.

You've written, "It was a beautiful day." What was beautiful about it? How did it make you or your character feel? What did it smell like? What did it sound like? Describe it. Take your skeletons and add flesh to them. Illuminate your scenes with detail and emotion.

11. Look for unintended meanings.

Could your sentence be read two different ways with two different meanings? For example: "The mayor spoke about sex with Harriet." Rewrite it so that we know whether the topic was sex with Harriet or whether the mayor spoke with Harriet and the topic was sex.

12. Watch for inconsistencies.

Is Darlene's dress green on page 112 and red five pages later? Did her eye or hair color change in mid-story without you noticing? Does Joe's name become John halfway through and Walter by the last chapter? Are Joe and Darlene indoors at the start of a scene and making a snowman (in mid-summer) at the end because you lost track of season and location?

A book, even an article or short story, is filled with details that can change from one section or draft to the next — sometimes intentionally, often not. After multiple drafts and read-throughs, these inconsistencies can be easy to miss. While reading, take notes of these details to keep them uniform.

13. Listen to your dialogue.

Listen to the rhythm and cadence of your characters' speech. Does it express their vision, profile and intent? Does it sound natural or forced? Listen to real people speaking — not to duplicate the content but to harmonize with the spirit. (Transcribe any unscripted conversation to see why you want your dialogue to be life*like* not true-life.)

14. Set your favorites free.

The sentence you love most, the description you think is unparalleled, the image you think is perfect: These are your favorites, and you may have an unhealthy attachment to them. View them objectively, from a place of loving detachment. Look at them in light of your vision. Ask yourself if they serve the larger work. If they don't, file them for later use. One may find a place in a future work. Another may be a powerful kickoff to a Muse Stream vignette, itself the potential spark for a longer piece.

15. Step into your reader's shoes.

What have you not explained to your reader? Are there holes in the narrative that ought to be filled? Ask yourself the same questions your reader will — and answer them.

16. Allow your readers their own experience.

What have you over-explained? Are you telling the reader too much? Your readers are smarter than you think. You don't need to explain every moment in your character's day. You don't need to describe every detail of every experience. You don't need to repeat "he said/she said" if only two people are speaking and the source of the quotes is clear.

17. You will make changes you regret.

To avoid losing the original, create a new document and printout for every draft. If you must make changes within a particular draft, keep the original text visible by enclosing your change in square brackets or by displaying it in a different color.

18. You will regret missing mistakes you could have corrected.

There will be errors you'll miss. There will be errors that editors and proofreaders will miss. Regardless of the number of times you read the manuscript and have it read by others, including by professionals, mistakes will slip through. When you discover them, note them so that you can correct future editions. Then let them go.

Seven More Rules for Revising Your Work

1. Be detached but loving.

Let your work sit quietly for a time before you launch into revision. That time could be a day, a week, a month or six months. And it could be longer or shorter from one piece of work to the next. The key is to give both you and your work the space and distance that allow you to approach it heartfully, objectively and discerningly. Respect your initial draft. Respect all your drafts. Don't be a slave to them. Allow your work to grow, change and mature.

2. Read aloud.

Whenever practical, read aloud. We are always more attuned to language, rhythm and flow when we read aloud. We often read more thoroughly when we read aloud. You will want to read your work silently as well, of course. But particularly at the beginning and each time you make major changes, your voice will tell you where you have strayed off course.

3. Be respectful, gentle and firm.

Treat each draft as you would your child — with love and without judgment. Revision is not about taking a broadaxe to your creation. It's about treating each draft as a necessary stage in its growth toward maturity. Just as you gently, sometimes firmly, guide your children toward the fulfillment of their unique destinies, guide your work with that same spirit of respect — for yourself as creator as well as for your creation, which has its own vision and imperative.

4. Accept that language is not perfect.

Do your best to bring your heart and vision to the page. Do your best to write the words and paint the images that most accurately reflect your dream and intention. As you revise, never hesitate to seek out more forceful and evocative ways to translate your vision onto the page. But remember that translation is an art and that language can rarely more than approximate emotion and experience. Think of the most wondrous scene you have ever witnessed and imagine trying to recreate that in words. You can come close. Yet whatever your mastery of the language, you will not recreate every nuance of your vision, emotion and experience. And that's okay.

5. Respect your intuition.

As you become more adept as a writer, more in tune with your work and its vision, and more in touch with your Muse, you will gain an intuitive knowingness of what works and what doesn't, without always being able to articulate why. That inner compass will direct you to the appropriate improvement or solution — again, often without explanation. Trust your intuition. It's the voice of your Muse, the voice of your vision. And it won't lead you astray.

6. Do your best.

Do your best to commit your vision to paper. Do your best to polish, enrich and enliven your work so that it aligns with that vision. Do your best on each piece of writing and, when it's time, let it go so that you can create a new work and do your best on that one as well.

7. Be the writer you are.

Each piece of writing will teach you, and from each piece of writing you will mature in your art and your craft. Strive for excellence not perfection. Be the writer you are.

You Are a Writer

Guided Meditation #10

For optimal results, record this guided meditation and play it back for your own use, or have a friend read it to you. A version recorded by the author is also available on The Voice of the Muse Companion CD *(see page 35).*

Close your eyes and take a few deep breaths as you relax and listen...

You are a writer. You are a writer of power, passion, strength and, yes, courage. For writing is an act of courage. Acknowledge that courage, the courage that got you to this point...having written. Having written today, if you have. Having written just now, if you have.

You are a writer. Breathe into that. Breathe into the release you felt as the pen flowed across the page, as letters formed into words, words stretched into sentences and sentences began to fill your pages.

Breathe into the freedom, the vibrancy, the love. Breathe into the knowledge and knowingness that you can do it again. And again. And again. And again.

You are a writer. What you write is powerful. What you write is vibrant. What you write, whatever you believe in this moment, is luminous.

Trust that to the best of your ability, in this moment. Acknowledge the writer you are, in this moment. Breathe into that.

Breathe out judgment. Breathe out fear. Breathe out not-good-enoughs. Breathe out comparisons. What others have written does not matter. What you have written is all that matters now, in this moment. It is perfect...in this moment. Know that. Trust that. Breathe into that.

If you don't feel ready to read what you have written from that place of trust, discernment and compassion, set it aside. Set it aside for a time — until you arrive at a place of more clarity, more objectivity, more self-love.

Don't avoid reading it, but nor do you need to rush into it. Either way, for now know that you are a writer. A writer writes. That's what you have done. You have written.

You are a *writer*.

You *are* a writer.

You are a writer.

You've heard the words. Now speak them with me...

I am a *writer*.

I *am* a writer.

I am a writer.

Speak them again and again and again, knowing them to be true. Speak them again, feeling the truth in them. Speak them again, for they are true.

14.

Creative Support

*It is not so much that we learn how to write
as that we learn how to trust ourselves.*

LAWRENCE BLOCK

*When you have the choice between being right
and being kind, always choose kind.*

WAYNE DYER

Sympathetic Vibrations

Feedback (noun): sympathetic vibration...
   — synonym in *Roget's International Thesaurus*, Sixth Edition, 2001

There is a time to hold your words and your work to yourself and a time to begin sharing them out into the world. Only you can know which time is which. Only you can decide how, when and with whom to begin the process.

Feedback is part of that sharing process. It involves selectively sharing your work in order to receive what will help you improve your writing and support you in your creativity. Selectively, because not everyone will be able to supply you with what you require, and not everyone will support you in the ways you need and desire.

Notice that I avoid words like "criticism" and "critique." For many people these words carry an emotional charge of harshness and negativity, even of cruelty. Words, as Alice discovered in Wonderland, bear the meanings we believe them to carry far more than they do their strict dictionary definitions. To me, "feedback" carries with it the potential of a positive, supportive response, of a sympathetic vibration.

Ultimately, however, the tone and tenor of any solicited response to your work is up to you. Do you want sympathetic vibrations or that other, less supportive definition of feedback, "unwanted noise"?

This is your work and your creative process. You have the right to full charge of both.

You have the right and the obligation to choose when you will seek feedback and from whom. You have the right and the obligation to choose the precise nature and level of feedback you will receive.

Remember, this is your creative journey. You cannot control it, but you can take charge of it and empower yourself in it. (See *Creative Connection*, page 221.)

How to Get Healthy Feedback

Stay in charge of your creative process by reading these guiding principles before sharing your work with anyone — including your life partner or best friend.

1. Be protective.

Your work is as much your creation as is your child. You have no more right to knowingly expose it to influences that could harm it or set it back than you do your child. Seek out only those people and situations that will support you and your writing. Never assume that the people closest to you — partner, parents, best friend — will be the most supportive. Always use your discernment.

2. Be open.

Your work, like your child, requires fresh air and outside influences. Don't be overprotective and suffocating. Be open to others' perceptions, comments and responses.

3. Be aware.

To everything there is a season. At different stages in your work and your process, you will be ready to hear different things. Respect where you are and seek only the type of feedback you are prepared to receive and integrate. Recognize when you are at your most raw and respect that.

4. Be clear.

Be clear about the type of feedback you require and desire. For example:

- Do you want to know what emotions your work evokes? Does it make her laugh? Does it make him cry?

- Do you want to know whether the reader found your descriptions, imagery or settings vivid and original? Whether your arguments were persuasive or convincing? Whether your dialogue was natural or appropriate?

- Do you want detailed line-by-line input?

- Do you want only general comments?

- Do you need a pat on the back for having completed a piece, or simply for having written?

5. Be explicit.

Once you know what kind of feedback is appropriate for you at this time, ask for it — clearly, directly and without equivocation. Your reader cannot know how best to support you unless you make your needs clear. Don't be shy or embarrassed to make those needs known. If you are vague and unclear, you open yourself to comments you are not ready to hear, comments that could feel damaging, even if they're not intended to be so.

6. Be strong.

Know what you want and don't be afraid to speak up — lovingly, forgivingly and compassionately — when you're not getting it, or when you're getting something you didn't ask for.

Remember, this is your work and your creative process. You have every right to be in charge. Remember, too: You are not only training yourself to seek out what will help and support you, you are training your friends and family to provide feedback in supportive ways, to provide sympathetic vibrations.

7. Be discerning.

The words on your page are an expression of you but they are not you. Negative comments, whether intentionally cruel or not, have no power to harm you, unless you abdicate your power and allow yourself to be hurt. In fact, take neither praise not criticism too seriously. Deep inside, you know your work's strengths and weaknesses. Tap into that inner knowingness and rely on it to discern which comments support you and serve your work at this stage in its development and yours.

How to Give Healthy Feedback

Share these guiding principles with those to whom you intend to show your work, and be certain they're comfortable abiding by them. Read them yourself before commenting on a friend's work.

1. Be nurturing.

Remember, the *only* reason to offer feedback is to support the writer and his or her work. This is not a test of your ability to pick out flaws. Don't be smart. Be gentle. Don't show off. Be fair.

2. Be balanced.

Always begin with the positive — with what you like about the piece, with its strengths, with what works for you. With that foundation of support, you can then begin to offer constructive comments. Remember, you can say anything you feel called to say about the work, as long as you frame it with respect and compassion.

3. Be specific.

You're at your most helpful when you can offer examples from the text of what works and what doesn't. Be clear.

4. Be respectful.

Give only the type and level of feedback the writer has sought. If there are other elements you would like to comment on, ask permission. Respect the answer you get.

5. Be compassionate.

Remember the Golden Rule of Feedback: "Speak unto others in the manner you would have them speak unto you." Put yourself in the writer's shoes and offer feedback as you would prefer to receive it.

Creative Connection

Too often, we don't recognize our creativity, can't see our talent, refuse to acknowledge our power. That's not surprising, given how solitary and insular writing can be, given how untrained so many people are in the words and actions that support creativity.

Groups are a powerful antidote to that. By coming together with other writers (yes, you *are* a writer!), you'll have an opportunity to take all you experience and read in these pages and multiply it manyfold through the loving support of others.

One way to forge creative connection and build creative support is by starting a Voice of the Muse Writers Circle. It's easy: Just share *The Voice of the Muse*, your enthusiasm and your commitment with a few like-spirited friends and writing colleagues and, voilà, you are part of a powerful vortex of motivation and inspiration.

However you format your Voice of the Muse Writers Circle, consider including these five elements:

1. Check-in

Set aside time for each member to share creative experiences since the last meeting. Here are some of the questions worth addressing: Are you writing? Is it easier to find time to write? Is writing getting easier? What have you written this week? What's happening with your submission?

Do your best to keep each contribution brief. This is not a time for mutual therapy; it's a time for mutual support. You want to make sure there's time for...

2. Creating

Set aside most of your time for writing and sharing. Pick or adapt an exercise from this book, create your own exercise or use a track from *The Voice of the Muse Companion CD* (see page 35). Then set a timer for fifteen, twenty or thirty minutes and write. When you're done, allow whoever wants to share what they have written that opportunity. Make sure everyone is familiar with the points in *How to Get/Give Healthy Feedback* (page 218 and page 220). In the beginning, focus more on general support than on detailed feedback.

3. Rotation

Take turns moderating the circle, hosting the circle and choosing the exercises.

4. Frequency

Agree to meet regularly, at least monthly.

5. Numbers

Keep the size of your group small enough so that everyone who wants to has an opportunity to share — if not at every meeting, then at every second or third meeting.

Here are some additional suggestions:

- Include a potluck as part of your get-together.

- Create creative space by using some of the suggestions in *Seven Tools for Transition*, page 142.

Remember, Voice of the Muse Writers Circles are designed to get you writing, keep you writing and support you in your creativity. Remember, too, that creativity at its best is a joyful experience. Write...and have fun!

15.

Living Your Creativity

*It is good to have an end to journey toward, but
it is the journey that matters in the end.*

URSULA K. LE GUIN

*The gods only go with you if you put yourself
in their path, and that takes courage.*

MARY STEWART

Leaps of Faith

You enter into this lifetime in the leap of faith your soul takes into the being in your mother's womb. You take that one huge leap only to discover that such leaps never cease being demanded of you.

The same is true with writing. Each project...each page...each word is another leap of faith, another leap into a void that calls you to it even as your natural, personality-mind instinct is to recoil.

But you do not. You move forward. You plow ahead. You let one word follow the one just written.

There is no uncertainty, for you know another word can and will always follow the one just completed — just as another moment will always follow the one just passed. It may not be the one you expected. It may not be the one your conscious mind would choose. Yet the word is there. And if, in the moment, it doesn't appear of its own volition, you can turn back to *Thirteen Rules for Writing* (page 30) to loosen the flow so that the word does emerge and the flow continues unchecked.

The same is true in life. If the flow stops, if you feel yourself pulled out of the present moment, you can do the life equivalent and stop to meditate, stop to write, stop to reconnect with the earth and the heavens, stop to find your grounding and centering. Stop to remember who you are. Stop to listen to the voice of your Muse, your soul, your heart. In that moment of cease you reconnect with the inner and again find your flow, again find your way.

To Everything There Is a Season

To everything there is a season. Nothing in nature matures overnight. Nothing in nature holds back its growth out of fear. Everything has its cycles and seasons.

Your act of creation is no different. It travels through a spiral that moves from silence back to silence, from blank page back to blank page, from completed work back to completed work. Each cycle's completion returns you not to where you began but to a higher level of awareness, mastery, openness and trust.

From silence to silence, word to word, trust to trust — the spiral is an infinite one, carrying you from one beginning to the next and one ending to the next on a journey with no beginning or ending.

It all begins, if a beginning we must choose, with a seed. You may have no awareness of this seed, planted deep in your unconscious. Yet there it sits, in a pod with many others, awaiting the right conditions for germination.

When you plant a seed in the earth, it moves into the realm of the invisible and you move into a place of trust. All you can do is water the spot on the earth above where you placed the seed. All you can do is create the right conditions and wait. All you can do is trust.

Trust that your idea, given the space, darkness and silence it needs, will germinate, like the seed, and begin to push fresh, fragile shoots toward the surface, toward the light.

Were you to deny your trust and dig down to prove its existence, you could well destroy it.

Let it be. Let yourself be. Sit in the silence. Accept the uncertainty. Open to the trust. Open to that unexpected moment when your green shoot of an idea bursts through to the light of your conscious mind.

"Aha!" you cry. "I have my story." And you do, or at least its beginnings.

There is a time to hold your new growth to yourself and a time to share it. Give your new creation, still in its genesis, the space to mature toward and onto the page. It is fragile and so, in your excitement, are you. Let your idea gain a few more shoots and let your heart and mind gain more confidence before you share it out into the world.

Others will know of it, in time.

Now is the time to channel your enthusiasm for your new growth toward its development. Now is the time to watch it blossom onto the page. Now is the time to transform your excitement into words, sentences and paragraphs.

Now is not the time to bring out the pruning shears or hedge cutters. How can you know what to trim when you have yet to see the direction of its growth? Give your plant the space to spread.

Give the writing its full time. Let your growing plant become what it needs to become, not what you would choose for it. When its shape emerges, when its vision and purpose become clear, then comes the time for judicious, but always loving, trimming and grafting.

Write now. Return later to revise. Later, when the writing is done, when the draft is complete.

One day your final draft will be done. It may not be as perfect as you would prefer, but it will be done. Your shoot is now a tree. You have done all you can to nurture it to maturity. More trimming and grafting would be counterproductive. It is strong enough to face your friends and neighbors — and you're strong enough to let it. It's time either to send it out into the world or file it away for future consideration. It's time to let it go.

It's time to return to the darkness.

If this were a circle, you would be back to the same place you began, as frustrated and uncertain as you were the first time, worried about your lack of ideas, for no ideas are immediately apparent.

But this is a spiral. When you leave your tree behind, when you complete your writing project, you have the benefit of your experience to guide you into the next one. You return to the darkness stronger and more confident. You know your tree will drop many seed pods into the earth and you trust that some will sprout in time. You know now that all you can do is create the right conditions and wait...and trust that from the waiting, from the darkness, something wondrous will emerge.

A spiral returns us not to our starting point, but to a place above it — to a new beginning at a heightened level of awareness and deeper level of trust and commitment.

Allow the spiral to carry you from word to word, project to project, season to season. And know that from each winter, you *will* emerge into the spring of new life, wiser, humbler and more aware of the cycles of all creation.

Here's a suggestion:

Where are you in your cycle of creation? Has your seed germinated? Or does it still sit in the realm of the invisible? Is it time to share your seedling with the world? Or do you and it both require additional growing time? Identifying your place in the spiral can free you to focus on where your project *is*, not on where you think it should be.

Your Words Are Your Teachers / *II*

Your words are your teachers. Don't run from your words any more than you would run from your teachers. Let them teach you all they have to teach you. Let them carry you to places you cannot yet imagine. Let them embrace you and protect you as they challenge you and push all the buttons you would rather they left untouched. Let them carry you on a journey of discovery, for that's what writing is: a journey that spirits you from unexpected word to unexpected word...to unexpected world.

Perhaps "discovery" is the wrong word. *Re*discovery is better, for through writing, you are becoming *re*acquainted with parts of yourself that you have forgotten so deeply you no longer suspect their presence.

Let writing reawaken those parts of you. Let it reignite the fire of your soul and give it expression as the flames form letters and words on the page or screen and, through that act, remind you of the depth of your beauty and the beauty of your depth.

Let your soul sing its song. Rediscover words you forgot you knew and free them to come racing through your heart and into your fingertips. Let your fingers create the marks on page or screen that give your soul's song permanence and life.

Surrender to the words. Surrender to the song. Surrender to the journey. Follow that journey wherever it takes you and I promise it will be a wondrous one. For all wonder flows from that act of surrender, of allowing, of letting go.

Surrender is not about giving up your soul or empowerment to someone or something else. It's about giving over your personality mind *to* your soul, *to* your empowerment. It's about experiencing your mystery and expressing your mastery. It's about living your creative potential — in your writing and in your life.

Here's a suggestion:

Explore what surrender means to you using any or all of these Muse Stream exercises. Set your timer for twenty minutes and write, without stopping, until the time is up.

- Write from this key phrase: "I surrender…"

- Write from this key phrase: "I surrender," she (or he) whispered…

- Create your own key phrase that contains the word "surrender."

- Write from the key word "surrender."

After you've written:

Did you write your *surrender* until the timer went off? Or until you sensed completion? Thank yourself for sticking with it. Know that what you wrote was powerful and important. Know that and don't judge it. Know that and own that power, in your writing and in your life.

Commit to Your Truth

The only rule, I wrote earlier, is that there are no rules. Perhaps there's a second notion that's worth turning into a rule: that you must enter into this journey prepared to trust, prepared to abandon all but your faith as you launch into this enterprise we call writing from the heart.

It is not a rule so much as a commitment, a commitment to follow your heart wherever it leads you.

There are no rules. Of course there aren't. But there is a commitment, to your truth and to its expression on the written page. That is why you are here, reading this book at this moment. Because you want to write. Because you want to write in a new way. Because you want to touch something true and authentic through your writing that you have not done before, or not done as easily before.

There is no need to struggle. There is only the need to trust. Your Muse will not let you down. If you don't believe in muses, then trust that the vision of your heart is so broad, so deep, so vast and so all-encompassing that it cannot let you down.

So place one word in front of the next, and then another and then another. Don't worry whether you are making sense. Don't worry whether you like what you've written. Don't worry at all. Just continue.

Continue past your judgment. Continue past your fear. Continue past your doubt. Continue past your hesitation. Continue past all that and you'll find yourself in a fairy land of truth. Not that you'll be writing fairy tales, but that you'll be in a place of such lightness you will not believe it. Either because the writing has come with such ease, perhaps for the first time, or because the heaviness that has weighed you down for so long has now moved through you and onto the page.

In giving it a physical form separate from your body, you have released the burden from your shoulders and back and can now walk upright, without stress. There is no call to stress. The only call is to be be. The only call is to write. The only call is to commit to your truth.

So, write your truth. Write it now.

What Matters Is the Journey

Are you impatient to get started? To get finished? Does your impatience serve as whip with which to beat yourself?

Instead, let your impatience help propel you forward. Let it be the engine pushing you beyond your boundaries. Let your impatience break down the walls and barriers that seemingly delay you.

Should that breakthrough not occur, don't look around for targets to apportion blame. Know instead that the path is not always smooth, the road is rarely straight and there is never one single itinerary to your destination. There are many roads, many paths, many means. All are valid. For there is no right or wrong. Even writing is not the only route. But it is the one to which you are called at this juncture.

Be in the moment with all your writing and know that you cannot make a mistake. Your personality mind may not always approve of the direction, but your heart will only grow and open more, regardless of the experience, as long as you approach it in that manner.

That's why there is no point in struggling for the right decision, any more than there is a point in struggling for the right word. Whichever word you allow, whichever path you surrender to will carry you to the destination you seek, the destination yearned for by your heart.

That is why writing from a key word or phrase is so effective, and such an effective metaphor for life's journey. Any starting point will do, for the destination will always be the same. What matters, in writing as in life, is the journey.

You cannot know where the journey will carry you. You cannot know and need not know. You can only know that your sole/soul choice is to embark on it and, wherever it carries you, to stay grounded in your truth.

Fly Free

Writing is a voyage of faith. There are no roads, no paths, save those you yourself trailblaze. No set of fixed directions save the one that calls you. Yes, it seems random. Yes, it can seem self-indulgent. But who else do you have to indulge during those precious moments of writing, connecting, receiving, recording?

Your imagination is limited by what you think you know. When you let go of that, when you leap off the bridge or cliff with nothing but trust, that's when you fly.

You doubt. Of course you do. Yet I guarantee you that if the level of your belief were such that you knew, in every cell and atom of your being, that you could fly, then you would. Until you do, direct your wings of faith to the written page, where, believe it or not, you can do yourself no harm. It may not always feel that way. It may feel dangerous. It is not. It is not and never has been.

All your feelings of danger are illusions, just as your inability to fly is an illusion. You can fly. But until you are able to fly off the bridge and soar to freedom, fly onto the page and experience your freedom that way.

Learn to love your freedom. Learn to love all that your freedom can bring you, teach you and show you. Share that freedom with others through your words. For freedom is what this book is about: the freedom to express who you are in every moment, fully trusting in your strength and creative power. What better way to test those wings of faith than on the page?

Let trust be your torch. Let faith light your way. Leap onto the blank page, with its lack of roads, paths, sequence, order or control. Let the words blaze the trail that only you can blaze, that only your words expressed in your unique manner can set forth. Then you *will* set forth, launched on the greatest journey imaginable: the journey of creation.

Now Is the Time

Do you know who you are? Do you know what you have chosen to be, the writer you have chosen to be? If so, then it's time to act on it. If you do, then as the explorer you are, it's time for you to brave the foreign lands of new emotions and fresh experiences and enter the world of your Muse.

Earlier in these pages, I encouraged you to not push yourself to write but to let the discipline of your heart guide your actions. I encouraged you to create the time and space, without forcing yourself into a fixed routine.

Now is the time to take the next step. Now is the time to commit, to commit to your Muse and through that to the writer you are.

Has a particular writing project revealed itself to you? Commit to it. If no project calls to you at this time, commit to the act of writing. Keep that fire of discipleship burning through your commitment.

The words are ready. Whether you feel ready or not, they are. Their readiness pushes you, too, to be ready. There is no more time to resist, to hesitate out of fear. Your work now is to light a fire with your words, to light the kind of fire you have never lit before.

As intensely as you have been inspired to pick up the pen and write, now it is time to stoke those flames. Your fire is now ready to roar and leap and ignite giant, powerful sparks. There is no time left for tentative wisps of light. Now is the time to blaze.

Now is the time to be committed. Now is the time to exercise that commitment. Now is the time to listen to the voice of the Muse, your Muse. Now is the time to take the words your Muse speaks to you alone and give them form, give them shape. Now is the time to devote yourself to the words that have for so long yearned to leap from your lips and fingertips. Now is the time.

Let the words out. Free those words that have labored so long within you. Now is the time.

Now is the time.

Now is the time to demonstrate a level of commitment and connection and compassion that you have never known or thought possible. Now is the time to say, "It does not matter what else is going on in my life. It does not matter who else is going on in my life. It does not matter whether I ever sleep again. It does not matter who is president or who is king. It does not matter whether I eat beans or caviar. None of this matters. What matters are the words that are ready to be birthed. What matters is that I honor them and myself and my Muse and every other human on this planet and every spirit and energy in this cosmos by setting those words free. That is my commitment."

You may think that I speak in extremes. It does matter, you say, whether you sleep or eat or love. Of course it does. I speak in extremes to make a point, to make the point that it has never been more important for you that the words within you be birthed onto the page.

The time to write is now. The time to write your truth is now. For by writing your truth, by tapping into the courage that allows you to do that, you will more fully *live* your truth. That is what is at stake. That is where your commitment is leading.

The time is now. The time to commit is now. The time to write is now. The time to free the words onto the page is now. The time to free yourself is now.

Be who you are. Live who you are. And discover your true depth and deepest truth through your words, through the words that are already backed up behind the dam of your fear, resistance and time-scarcity consciousness. The time is there, if you but believe it. The time is there if you but release your martyrdom around it. The time is there. Believe it and act on it.

You do not like the restriction of discipline? Too bad. It is time to be a disciple to your Muse and, through that commitment, not a commitment to victimhood, be truly disciplined.

Connect with the energy of your writing daily — on your book or project or, until that materializes, any heartful words set to paper.

Your best method, though not necessarily the only one, is through writing. Sit down and write. Meditate. Visualize. En-vision.

If you have been called to write a book, you may know something of its form and content. You may know nothing. It's time now to discover what you do not know. In the discovery, you will gain your material for that book.

Even if what you're writing isn't a book, following that same journey of discovery will reawaken your Muse, will reawaken you.

Continue. Daily. Continue daily so as not to lose the energetic thread you are spinning. Write daily through any and all upheavals, fears, fatigues. Write daily through any and all mishaps, challenges and mistakes. Let that be your commitment. Through that commitment, your book *will* take shape. For you will remain connected to its energetic thread and will allow that thread to weave itself into the wondrous tapestry it already is.

Whatever you're writing, make a commitment, now at this moment, to spend time with it every day.

Of course, it may not always be possible to sit down and write every day. Other commitments, responsibilities and obligations will intrude from time to time.

It doesn't matter. If you cannot sit down and write, connect in some other concrete way. Let the silences, as few as they are throughout your day, speak to you of your writing, your project, your book.

Stay connected. To your Muse. To your heart. To yourself.

Make that commitment. Make it now.

Here's a suggestion:

Speak this statement of commitment aloud, making it your own. Speak it, and live up to it.

Statement of Commitment

I, [*your name*], commit myself to my writing
[and to *name of your book/project*].

I commit to answering the call to write, by writing.

I commit myself to keeping the connection with my writing
[and with *name of your book/project*] open, alive
and free, every day.

And so it is.

The Voice of Your Muse

Welcome to the book of knowledge that lies within you — not so far below the surface as once it lay. Welcome to your story as it unreels and unravels onto the page, onto the page of life that transcends so many dimensions.

You are a writer. Never doubt that for an instant. Never doubt that what you write has the potential to touch millions, to transform not only this planet but the entire cosmos.

It doesn't matter whether your words ever move beyond the privacy of your page or screen. It doesn't matter for they have already changed you. And in changing you they change the world.

Open to them. Open to them and release all expectations. Let the fearful parts of you know that they are loved but that they are not and cannot be in charge.

Let go of all attachments and expectations. Let go of all attachments to the story as you believe it must or should be. Let go of all attachments to outcomes, be they related to the story's end or the manuscript's fate.

Let go all of that and focus your energy, will, desire and calling into this moment, into this word...and now this one. For this word is the one that will change you. And this word...and this one.

See yourself as the word. See yourself as the word made manifest and know that every word in your story, article, poem, book, journal entry... life...is like that: a word that floats within you, unformed in the physical until you as God and Creator say, "Let it have form. Let it have letters. Let it be made physical. Let it have structure. Not the structure I choose for it, but the structure it chooses for itself. Let it have shape. Not the shape I choose for it, but the shape it chooses for itself."

Let it have a life, an imperative, a calling. Not the one you would choose for it, but the one that flows and derives naturally from its heart and your own.

You are a writer, you who read these words today. You are a writer, you who doubt your abilities, talents and creative capacity.

Perhaps you doubt them not in this moment. Are there moments when you do? Breathe through those moments and keep on. Keep going, keep writing, keep allowing the forces of creation to move through you with the force of your beating heart, the force of your spirit, the force of the cosmos that exists whole and unedited within you.

You are all there is and all that is, Creator of your universe...in life as much as on the page.

So write. Write the healing, write the wrongs, write the life and write the love. And know that through all your creative endeavors, as through all your life endeavors, your Muse is with you, waiting for the opening in your mind and heart that will free its creative power into your life.

Go now. Listen to the voice of your Muse...and write.

Now.

16.
Parting Words

Why, sometimes I've believed as many as six impossible things before breakfast.

LEWIS CARROLL

If God gives you something you can do, why in God's name wouldn't you do it?

STEPHEN KING

The Story Knows

As I sit writing this on a late summer morning in 2002, I'm perched on a slab of Sedona red rock, high above a desert canyon.

Before me, Thunder Mountain's bichromatic cliffs of crimson and cream soar up into the clouds. Behind me, Chimney Rock pokes its eons-eroded phallus into the morning sky.

I was pulled inexorably toward this magnificent red-rock aerie — not knowing where the trail was carrying me, nor why. Not knowing, that is, until I sat down, gazed across at Sedona's majestic splendor, and felt these words pour through me.

When I began writing this book in Hawaii, I could not have imagined being here...could not have imagined wanting to be here. Yes, I had lived in Sedona before, had loved Sedona before. Here is where I met my wife and here is where we conceived our daughter. How could I not love this place?

Yet when the call came to leave for Hawaii, our attachment to Sedona dissolved. From that moment until another, three and a half years later, we never looked back, never believed we would live any place other than somewhere on that strand of Pacific pearls.

The Big Island and then Maui threw many challenges at us. But the mana, or spirit, of that sacred land, along with the aloha spirit I referred to earlier in these pages, left us convinced we would never leave.

Yes, there were times when we talked of leaving. On those days, either the transformative force of the islands or man's polluting assaults on them seemed more painful than I could bear. Even in those moments, Sedona rarely surfaced as an option.

Then one day the red rocks called us back...softly at first, then with increasing insistence. We tried not to listen. We insisted that Maui was our home, that we lacked the funds to consider such a move.

We insisted and resisted until finally we surrendered — and watched all that was required to get us back to Sedona fall effortlessly into place.

Now I sit on this rocky slab, awed not only by the transcendent beauty of this spot but by the perfection of my personal story, a story whose next chapter I could not have begun to imagine.

Writing is like that. We have an idée fixe about our story and where it should go. When the story suggests another route, we often fight it, insisting that we know best.

The story always knows best. Always.

There's another reason I was drawn to this spot. It has a particular symbolism for me — and, possibly, for you.

Writing is often a solitary act. It's not unusual for what we write to remain buried forever in a computer file or between the covers of a notebook or journal.

Thunder Mountain and Chimney Rock are alive with masculine power, with the energy of being present out in the world. It's an energy potential we all carry, whatever our gender. Thunder Mountain, in fact, is an integral part of Sedona's skyline, visible from almost anywhere in town.

Being here, sandwiched between these two mighty rocks, reminds me to let my voice thunder from the mountaintops. It reminds me to let the procreative power of my words be felt in far distant places. It reminds me to come out of hiding and allow myself to be seen and known.

Yes, writing can be a solitary act. But there is a time to seed creation, transformation and healing. There is a time to thunder your message of love and wisdom up and out into the world.

That time is now.

It's time now for you to gift others with your courage, strength and aloha...with your words.

As for me, I'm grateful to have rediscovered this forum for my thunder as I, too, open to my heart and to the next chapter in my story.

Here's a suggestion:

Share your words out into the world. If you can't yet thunder them from a mountaintop, start by reading them aloud to yourself in front of a mirror. Graduate to sharing them with a trusted friend, one who will listen in support, not judgment. (Share *Creative Support*, Chapter 14, with that friend.) Expand your sharing by starting a Voice of the Muse Writers Circle (see *Creative Connection*, page 221). Move on to an open mic night at your local café, or to an e-mail transmission to friends and family.

Thunder your truth, in whatever way you can, in whatever way represents the next step in your coming-out. Take that risk, recognizing that whispering the words of your heart into a mirror can sometimes be as soul-baring as shouting them from a soapbox on Main Street.

The Story Knows Best

The next chapter of my life didn't play out as I expected when writing the previous piece. Two years later, my marriage ended and I again found myself on the sort of open-ended road trip I wrote about in *Surrender to the Journey* (page 43).

This time, my journey — from Sedona, not to it — took me across the continent not once but multiple times, on a voyage that lasted thirty months not three.

This time, I landed not among the red rocks of northern Arizona but on the high-desert slopes of Albuquerque's Sandia Mountains.

Yet in most other ways, the parallel with my 1997 odyssey is complete: Like all of us, I am in the midst of a story that is still being written and whose ending has yet to be revealed.

As I move into the next chapter of my life here in New Mexico, I am reminded that this, like all journeys, is one of infinite surrender — word by word, moment by moment, breath by breath. I am particularly reminded of this as I reflect on where I wrote the first draft of this piece: in Santa Fe, a city whose name translates as "holy faith."

In this moment I cannot tell you how this chapter will end nor where the next will take me, just as I cannot yet know where *The MoonQuest*'s sequel, *The StarQuest*, will go as I return to its pages.

All I can do — all we can ever do, in writing as in life — is trust in the story.

It has never let me down before.

Truly, the story knows best.

Here's a suggestion:

Surrender to *your* journey. Open your mind to those parts of your story you have not allowed yourself to see — both on your page and in your life. Allow yourself to experiment with new forms, new genres, new paper, new pens. Venture out onto the ledge of your consciousness and creativity and take the leap that will transform the world — beginning with your own.

The Envelope, Please!

Do you remember the questions I asked you to answer when you first opened *The Voice of the Muse*?

It's time to retrieve that sealed envelope from the back of this book. Open it, pull out the pieces of paper or index cards and read what you wrote. Read it now. Reacquaint yourself with where you believed yourself to be last week...last month...last year...whenever you started this book.

Are you surprised? Has anything changed? Has everything changed?

Turn over your card/paper or get a fresh one and ask yourself these questions:

- Where am I now?

- Where am I now in my writing? In my life?

- Where am I now at the end of this book?

Close your eyes and let a single word, phrase or sentence emerge that describes where you are in this moment. Don't judge it. Surrender to it, whatever it is, and then write it under today's date next to the question, "Where am I now?"

Now, write a few lines describing where you are today with your writing, with your creative journey. What did you accomplish and achieve over the course of our time together? What has changed since you wrote those first words all those pages ago? How has your Muse spoken to you? What has your Muse said? What has your Muse given you?

Write that and send me a copy if you like (c/o LightLines Media or my web site: www.markdavidgerson.com). Then open your heart to the voice of your Muse...and keep writing!

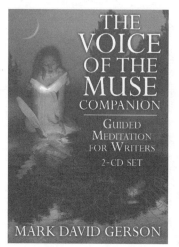